ROUTLEDGE LIBRARY EDITIONS:
MACROECONOMICS

Volume 9

ECONOMIC GROWTH

ECONOMIC GROWTH

Analysis and Policy

W. A. ELTIS

Routledge
Taylor & Francis Group
LONDON AND NEW YORK

First published in 1966 by Hutchinson & Co (Publishers) Ltd

Published in 2016 by Routledge
2 Park Square, Milton Park, Abingdon, Oxon OX14 4RN
52 Vanderbilt Avenue, New York, NY 10017

Routledge is an imprint of the Taylor & Francis Group, an informa business

British Library Cataloguing in Publication Data
A catalogue record for this book is available from the British Library

ISBN: 978-1-138-93746-8 (Set)
ISBN: 978-1-315-67362-2 (Set) (ebk)
ISBN: 978-1-138-94479-4 (Volume 9) (hbk)
ISBN: 978-1-315-67167-3 (Volume 9) (ebk)

ECONOMIC GROWTH

ANALYSIS AND POLICY

W. A. Eltis

Fellow of Exeter College, Oxford

HUTCHINSON UNIVERSITY LIBRARY

LONDON

HUTCHINSON & CO (*Publishers*) LTD
178–202 Great Portland Street, London W1

London Melbourne Sydney
Auckland Bombay Toronto
Johannesburg New York

★

First published 1966

This book has been set in Times, printed in Great Britain by Benham and Company Limited, Colchester, on Smooth Wove paper, and bound by Wm. Brendon and Son Limited of Tiptree, Essex

CONTENTS

Preface 7

1 Investment, technical progress, and economic growth 9
Mathematical Appendix 31

2 Research and technical progress 35
Appendix: The 'neutrality' of technical progress 43

3 Capital intensity and economic growth 45
Appendix I: The rate of profit, and relative prices of capital and consumer goods 63
Appendix II: The 'Cobb–Douglas' production function 66

4 Economic growth at full employment 71

5 Government policy for growth: I Policy to control the overall rate of investment 98

6 Government policy for growth: II Policy to influence capital intensity 129

7 Growth and the balance of payments 148

8 Conclusion 166

Index 171

PREFACE

In Sir Roy Harrod's words, 'Economic growth is the grand objective. It is the aim of economic policy as a whole'.[1] With faster growth, most economic problems can be solved more quickly and easily, and the people of a country can generally enjoy higher living standards, or better social services, or give more aid to the people of other countries. It should be noted, however, that a change from a slower to a faster rate of growth may require a temporary fall in the rate of increase of consumption.

This book is concerned with the theory of economic growth, and its relevance to policy for growth in developed economies. In the first three chapters, the various factors which determine the potential growth rate of a developed economy are considered and analysed. In Chapters 4–6, the problems involved in actually achieving growth at the potential rate with continuous full employment are considered. Finally, in Chapter 7, the problem of combining growth at the potential rate with a satisfactory balance of payments is discussed; this chapter forms an indispensable part of the argument, because growth and the balance of payments cannot be considered in isolation, as the recent experience of the UK demonstrates.

Since 1963, I have spent part of my time in the National Economic Development Office, and I have found discussions there on many of the problems considered in this book most stimulating and helpful. I should make it clear that the detailed argument of the book is entirely my own, and it should not be presumed that the policy outlined is necessarily favoured or advocated by the National Economic Development Office.

I am grateful to Mr J. Black, Mr J. Boulter, Mr E. B. Butler,

[1] *Reforming the World's Money*, Macmillan, 1965, p. 77.

Mr D. O. Faulkner, Sir David Henderson-Stewart, Mr B. Reading, Mr G. B. Richardson, Mr M. Rudd, Mr M. FG. Scott, and Professor J. N. Wolfe for helpful comments on various chapters. The responsibility for any errors that remain is entirely mine.

I am grateful to the editors of *Oxford Economic Papers* for permission to reprint a revised version of an article, which appeared there, as Chapter 1 of the present book.

Finally, I owe a particular debt to Sir Roy Harrod who has read and commented on all the chapters. This book could not have been written without his encouragement and advice.

Exeter College
Oxford

W.A.E.

I

INVESTMENT, TECHNICAL PROGRESS, AND ECONOMIC GROWTH

Introduction

Growth in the productive capacity of a developed economy is inevitable. There will be continuous additions to its technical knowledge as a result of research and new discoveries; so it will often become possible for it to produce goods with fewer workers, less capital, or less of some other factor of production. The output of a developed economy with given factor supplies will then be able to rise from year to year.

Moreover, a developed economy is likely to add to its capital through continuous net investment. In developed economies, the amount of capital is almost always increased more quickly than population; so capital per worker rises most of the time, and any addition to capital per worker must raise potential output.

These additions to capital and to technical knowledge will either increase or permit increases in its productive capacity. Its output (as well as its productive capacity) will then be able to grow, provided that demand for its goods rises continuously.

The effects of what are now regarded as quite moderate rates of growth are very startling indeed if they can be maintained for a century. An increase in output per worker of 2% per annum would amount to an increase of 624% in a century, while an increase of 4% per annum would amount to 4,912% in a century. As Keynes pointed out, the combined effects of increases in knowledge, increases in capital, and compound interest can be very powerful.[1]

Two elementary approaches to the determination of the rate of

[1] J. M. Keynes, 'The economic possibilities for our grandchildren', *Essays in Persuasion*, Macmillan, 1931.

growth focus simply on the increase in capital or the increase in technical knowledge. The approach which attributes growth solely to investment and the quantity of capital will be explained first.

Investment and economic growth—the $\frac{S}{C}$ *formulation*

Through investment, new capital is installed in an economy each year, and this increases its productive capacity. If there was no investment, everything produced would be consumed, capital would gradually wear out, and production would fall from year to year. A certain amount of investment is needed to prevent production from falling, and the investment needed for this can be defined as 'investment needed to cover depreciation', or simply 'depreciation'. Investment in excess of 'depreciation' is *net* investment, and total or *gross* investment then equals 'depreciation' plus *net* investment. It follows from this definition of *net* investment that all *net* investment raises net output, since depreciation keeps net output constant, and any investment in addition to this must raise net output.

If S% of an economy's net output (referred to subsequently as Net National Product or NNP) consists of net investment, S% of its NNP will be used to make net additions to its capital. With a capital output ratio of new capital of C, net investment of £C would add £1 to the following year's NNP, because £C worth of new capital would produce £1 worth of output per annum. Net investment of £1 would then add £$\frac{1}{C}$ to the following year's NNP, and the total net investment made in a year, S% of the NNP altogether, would add $\frac{S\% \text{ of NNP}}{C}$ to net output in the following year. Since output in the following year would then be higher by NNP times $\frac{S}{C}$%, the rate of growth of the NNP would be $\frac{S}{C}$% in the year concerned, where S is the percentage of the NNP consisting of net investment, and C is the capital output ratio of new capital.[1]

[1] This formula was originated by Sir Roy Harrod in 'An essay in dynamic theory', *Economic Journal*, 1939.

If S equalled 12% of the NNP, and the capital output ratio of new capital was 4, the rate of growth of the NNP would be $\frac{12}{4}\%$ or 3% per annum. If the NNP was originally 100, 12 of the 100 units produced in the first year are net investment, and can be added to the economy's stock of capital. Every 4 of these units of capital can produce a unit of net output a year; so the following year's output will be the original 100 units, plus a quarter of 12 units, or 103 units altogether—a growth rate of 3% per annum from the previous year's 100 units. The growth rate would remain 3% for as long as S remained 12% and C 4. If S became higher than 12% the rate of growth would rise, while it would fall if C became higher than 4.

If C is defined as the increase in capital actually made in a particular period divided by the increase in output which actually occurs in that period, the S/C formulation is a tautology.[1] Sometimes, however, C is not defined as the actual capital output ratio, but a value of C derived from past experience is used to estimate the effect on the *future* rate of growth of a particular rate of investment. For instance, Professor W. Fellner wrote in 1956 of the USA: 'It is quite conceivable that by doubling net capital formation our growth rate could be fully doubled.'[2] Here the argument that a doubling of S would quite conceivably double the rate of growth implies that doubling S would leave C unaltered.

Capital per worker rises continuously in an economy with full employment, and an increased share of investment in the NNP would increase the rate at which it rose. It is well known that 'When, in a given state of knowledge, factors of production which are in variable supply are added to another factor of production

[1] See R. F. Harrod, op. cit. If C is defined as the $\frac{\text{net increase in capital}}{\text{net increase in output}}$ over a given period of time, S as the $\frac{\text{net increase in capital}}{\text{net output}}$ in the same period of time, and the rate of growth in this period of time as $\frac{\text{net increase in output}}{\text{net output}}$, $\frac{S}{C}$ equals $\frac{\text{net increase in capital}}{\text{net output}}$ divided by $\frac{\text{net increase in capital}}{\text{net increase in output}}$ which equals $\frac{\text{net increase in output}}{\text{net output}}$ which is identically equal to the rate of growth.

[2] Professor W. Fellner, *Trends and Cycles in Economic Activity*, Holt, New York, 1956, p. 74.

which is in fixed supply, the marginal products of the variable factors eventually diminish'. According to this principle, if there was a *given state of knowledge*, increases in capital per worker would eventually lead to a lower marginal product of capital, i.e., to a higher marginal capital output ratio, a higher C, and therefore to a slower rate of growth from a given share of investment. Because there is not a *given state of knowledge* in any actual economy, since knowledge about methods of production is added to continuously, certain additions to capital per worker can be made each year without bringing the point of diminishing returns nearer. There is the further possibility that the point where diminishing returns to capital would begin might be distant in some economies because of a large backlog of unexploited investment opportunities, and capital per worker could then be increased rapidly for many years without a rise in C.[1] When a past value of C is extrapolated into the future, it is implicitly assumed that either technical progress, or a large backlog of unexploited investment opportunities would prevent C from rising in the period of the prediction.

If there is not full employment in an economy there is no reason why there should be diminishing returns to capital, and there is then no reason why C should rise when S is increased. In such an economy, doubling S would be much more likely to double the rate of growth. It is also evident that with unemployment a given amount of *gross* investment would add more to *gross* output than it would with full employment. Suppose a machine costs £3,000, requires one worker to work it, and adds £1,500 a year to gross output. In an economy with unemployed workers, one of these could work the machine and there would be an addition to gross output of £1,500. In an economy with full employment a worker would have to be taken from other work where he was producing output worth, say, £800 a year (with an older machine) to work the new machine. In this economy gross output per year would be increased by £1,500 less £800, or by £700.[2] Thus identical

[1] The circumstances where this would occur are considered in detail below.

[2] If the economy with full employment installed a great deal of capital of this type, after a time it would run out of workers who were only adding £800 to gross output, and it would need to use workers adding perhaps £900 each to gross output to work the new machinery. The addition to gross output from investment of £3,000 in this kind of machine would then fall from £700 to £600, which illustrates part of the process through which a faster rate of investment does not raise the rate of growth in the same proportion when there is full employment.

investments would add £1,500 to gross output in one economy and £700 in the other.

The S/C formulation would be affected in the following way by these investments. The capital output ratios of the machines themselves would be much the same in both economies, so the C's due to the investments would be similar. On the other hand, since the depreciation of capital is 'whatever amount of investment is needed to keep net output constant', the fall of £800 in the output of old capital in the economy with full employment would raise depreciation in that economy (by an amount approximately equal to the cost of the capital needed to produce £800 worth of output) and consequently reduce its S, while the S of the economy with unemployment would not be reduced. Thus the growth resulting from investment in this type of machine would be less in an economy with full employment because the latter would have more depreciation, a lower S, and therefore a lower S/C. If the types of capital installed in the two economies differed, capital with a higher capital output ratio would probably be installed in the economy with full employment (because of labour scarcity, and its effect in raising capital intensity), and this too would reduce its S/C.

It would consequently be particularly inaccurate to try to predict the growth rate which would follow from a greater share of gross investment in the Gross National Product of an economy with full employment by looking at the effect on the rate of growth of a similar share of gross investment in an economy with unemployment. An argument, for instance, that the UK's growth rate in the 1960's would be the same as West Germany's in the 1950's if the UK invested the same proportion of her GNP as West Germany invested in the 1950's, would be particularly inaccurate for this reason.

The S/C formulation is a truism if it refers to the past, and it can only be used safely to help to predict the future growth rates which would follow from particular investment policies if there is either sufficient unemployment, or sufficient technical progress, or a sufficient backlog of unexploited investment opportunities to prevent diminishing returns to capital in the period of the prediction.

Technical progress and the 'natural' rate of growth

An alternative formulation of the problem[1] attributes growth

[1] See R. F. Harrod, *Towards a Dynamic Economics*, Macmillan, 1948, pp. 20–4.

almost entirely to technical progress and population increase. It is assumed throughout this section and the next that demand is always maintained at a level just sufficient to permit the full employment of labour,[1] that the supply of finance is infinitely elastic at the ruling rate of interest, i.e., that any entrepreneur can borrow as much as he wishes at the ruling rate of interest provided he can give adequate security; and that investment is always pushed to the limit of profitable opportunity. Then, through competition, entrepreneurs would push investment to the point where their expected profit rate from investment exceeded the interest rate by a margin sufficient to cover risk. The profit rate would then always exceed the interest rate by the risk premium that entrepreneurs required.

The importance of technical progress and population increase is best seen if a situation is envisaged where both are absent. It is supposed that there is a labour force of constant size and that there are no additions to technical knowledge. There would then be certain known ways in which capital could be used to raise output. If the rate of interest was initially 5%, for instance, and the risk premium 3%, so that entrepreneurs required an expected profit rate of 8% from investment, only those uses of capital which were expected to raise the value of net output by more than 8% of the cost of the capital required could possibly be worth undertaking, and when all the investment projects which were expected to yield more than 8% had been carried out, net investment would fall to zero. If the rate of interest fell to 4% there would be some further investment opportunities which could be expected to yield 7%, but in time these too would be exhausted. If the rate of interest then fell to the lowest possible level, net investment would fall permanently to zero after all the investment projects which were expected to yield the rate of profit corresponding to that interest rate had been carried out.

It is now supposed that the rate of interest is constant, that there is given technical knowledge as before, but that the labour force increases by 1% each year. If labour and capital were the only factors of production, it would be profitable to extend every kind of capital installation by 1% each year (if capital was infinitely divisible), and, with the extra 1% of labour, raise output by 1% each year; and if capital was not infinitely divisible, to extend

[1] The problems involved in this will be considered in detail in Chapters 4 and 5.

capital and raise output by an average of 1% a year over a period of years. If there were possible economies of scale, it would be profitable to expand output by more than 1% a year, while if factors of production other than labour and capital were needed, and some of these were in scarce supply, it might be unprofitable to expand output by as much as 1% a year because of diminishing returns. One per cent would be the order of magnitude of the annual increase in output which would be profitable, and a limited amount of investment would be needed each year to produce the extra output.

It is now supposed that the size of the labour force is constant, that the rate of interest is constant, but that there are additions to technical knowledge each year. An advance in technical knowledge could be defined as 'new knowledge which would either permit existing products to be produced at lower cost,[1] or which would permit the production of new products'. By taking advantage of an advance in knowledge, entrepreneurs would earn higher profits than their competitors until all entrepreneurs manufacturing the goods in question used the new method of production. Some new methods of production require investment, and this would of course be the case if the new method was made possible by the development of superior machinery. Such advances are usually referred to as 'embodied' technical progress, because the advance in knowledge has to be *embodied* in new machinery. As soon as the new machinery came into use, the price of the product would begin to fall relatively to the costs of production of entrepreneurs not using it (through competition), and their profits would consequently fall. In time, a point would be reached where it would pay them to scrap their old machinery and replace it with machinery incorporating the new knowledge.[2] Because of such staggering of investment, an advance in knowledge requiring the use of new capital would normally permit profitable investment

[1] New knowledge might permit lower costs and therefore constitute an advance with one rate of interest, while with a different rate of interest it would not permit production at lower cost, and would not therefore constitute an advance at that rate of interest. This problem is avoided here because it is assumed that the rate of interest is constant.

[2] The traditional view is that this point is reached when cost per unit of output with the new method of production is less than cost per unit *excluding capital cost* with existing machinery. The discovery of this point requires entrepreneurial judgement and not merely accountancy, because the economic life of the new capital has to be estimated before the cost of production with the new method can be calculated.

stretching over many years. Other advances in knowledge might simply require a rearrangement of existing factors of production, and these would permit reductions in cost without investment. Advances in knowledge of this kind are usually referred to as 'disembodied' technical progress. It would pay entrepreneurs to take advantage of 'disembodied' technical progress immediately. All reductions in cost could lead to increases in total output because the factors of production released could be used elsewhere in the economy. For instance, any cost reductions which permitted economy in the use of labour would release workers, and it would then be potentially profitable to extend capital throughout the economy with the consequences which were analysed above. Through the replacement of capital and the redeployment of labour, advances in knowledge of all kinds would permit a certain increase in output each year. A certain amount of investment would be needed to obtain the full increase in output made possible by advances in knowledge each year, but only this amount of investment could be made profitably at a given rate of interest.

Either a fall in the rate of interest, or an increase in the size of the labour force, or an advance in technical knowledge permits an increase in output, and when investment is always pushed to the limit of profitable opportunity, these together determine the rate of growth of output. If the effect of changes in the rate of interest is disregarded, the rate of growth would depend on the increase in the labour force and advances in technical knowledge alone. If, for instance, the growth of the labour force made an increase in output of p% a year possible, and technical progress made an increase in output of t% a year possible, criteria of profitability would permit an increase in output of approximately (t+p)% each year. Sir Roy Harrod has called 'the rate of advance which the increase of population and technological improvements allow', the 'natural' rate of growth,[1] and this rate of (t+p)% is the 'natural' rate of growth.

If the 'natural' rate of growth was, for instance, 3% a year, and the capital output ratio of the new capital required averaged 4, it would be profitable to add four times 3% or 12% of the NNP to the capital stock. In this case S would equal 12%, C would be 4, and S/C would equal 3%, the 'natural' rate of growth. The growth in output of 3% a year would be made possible by technical progress and population increase, and the net investment of 12% of the NNP would simply be needed to realise this potential increase in

[1] R. F. Harrod, *Towards a Dynamic Economics*, p. 87.

output. If investment was 13% of the NNP, the thirteenth per cent would be unprofitable,[1] while if less than 12% of the NNP was invested, output would rise by less than the possible 3%.

The 'full natural' rate of growth

So far it has been assumed that the rate of technical progress which (with the rate of increase of the labour force) determines the 'natural' rate of growth does not depend at all on the rate of investment, and the rate of expansion of output. Investment was simply needed to take advantage of such technical progress as occurred, but it did not itself influence the rate of technical progress. Because the development of superior methods of production is both more profitable and more practicable when the rate of investment is high,[2] it could be argued that there might be some connection between the share of investment in the National Product and the rate of technical progress.[3] If technical progress

[1] It might appear at first sight that if the rate of profit corresponding to a particular interest rate was r%, and investment was pushed to the limit of profitable opportunity, the marginal productivity of capital would be r%. A marginal investment of £100 would then add just £r to net output; so the marginal capital output ratio would be 100:r. Unprofitable investment, i.e., investment in excess of that needed to realise the 'natural' rate of growth, would then have a marginal productivity of less than r%, and therefore a marginal capital output ratio of more than 100:r, and the contribution to the rate of growth of an extra 1% of the NNP which was invested (extra to that needed for the 'natural' rate) would then be less than r/100%. This would follow exactly if there was perfect competition in all markets, constant returns to scale, and no change in the rate of interest. With increasing returns to scale, or imperfect competition, the marginal productivity of capital would exceed r%; so a marginal investment of £100 would increase net output by more than £r. If the extra investment was accompanied by a lower interest (and corresponding profit) rate, the cost of capital might alter relative to the prices of its products which would also affect the calculation. (This complication is considered in detail in Appendix I to Chapter 3.)

[2] If the rate of investment is high, a greater quantity of a new kind of machine can be sold which permits the use of more economies of scale in its manufacture, which reduces its cost and so encourages users of machinery to purchase machinery which formerly had a higher capital output ratio. The development of technically superior machinery would also be more profitable to manufacturers of machinery. A high output of machinery might also accelerate the eradication of weaknesses in the design and performance of new machinery. These points have all been made by Professor N. Kaldor.

[3] See Professor N. Kaldor's, 'A model of economic growth', *Economic Journal*, 1957, 'Capital accumulation and economic growth' in *The Theory of Capital*, edited by F. A. Lutz and D. C. Hague, Macmillan, 1961, and 'A new model of economic growth' (with James A. Mirrlees), *Review of Economic Studies*, 1962.

depended on investment, it would be more likely to depend on gross investment than on net investment, because all investment would be likely to contribute to it. There would be some technical progress even if gross investment (in capital goods) was zero (due to the forces influencing technical progress which are independent of investment such as research in the universities, in government research institutions, and in business research departments which are not closed down in depressions, and improvements spontaneously discovered by workers and managements), and the technical progress in addition to this would depend on the amount of gross investment, or, it could be supposed, on the share of gross investment in the National Product.

Then, if net investment was zero, there would be technical progress due to the research which continued whether there was investment or not, and additional technical progress due to the gross investment which would be needed to cover depreciation. If, for instance, the technical progress from these two sources together amounted to 2% per annum, the rate of technical progress would be 2% per annum when net investment was zero. If the additional technical progress which was due to investment was, for instance, 1% per annum for every 6% of S (the share of net investment in the NNP),[1] the rate of technical progress would be 2% plus 1% for every 6% of S. The rate of technical progress would then be 2% per annum when S was zero, 4% per annum when S was 12%, and 6% per annum when S was 24%. Doubling S from 12% to 24% would then increase the rate of technical progress from 4% to 6% (i.e., it would be less than doubled), and the $\frac{S}{C}$ formulation would not predict future growth rates accurately, because doubling S would not induce enough extra technical progress to overcome diminishing returns.

If the rate of interest was given, and there was a capital output ratio which was most profitable at the profit rate corresponding to that interest rate, the rate of growth would tend towards one particular 'natural' rate of growth if entrepreneurs pushed investment

[1] When S is higher, the amount of investment which is needed to cover depreciation is also higher (because more workers have to be transferred from old capital to work new capital, and the annual fall in the output of old capital is consequently greater), and the extra technical progress of 1% for each 6% of S is due, both to the net investment of 6%, and to the extra investment which is needed in consequence to cover higher depreciation, because it depends on the share of gross investment in the National Product.

to the limit of profitable opportunity. If, for instance, the most profitable capital output ratio was 3, S would tend towards 12% where both the actual and the 'natural' rates of growth would be 4%. If S was less than 12%, the actual rate of growth would be less than the 'natural' rate, so entrepreneurs would find it profitable to increase S, while if S was more than 12%, the 'natural' rate of growth would be insufficient to allow the investment in excess of 12% to be profitable, and S would fall to 12%. If there was a lower interest rate and corresponding profit rate, and the most profitable capital output ratio was consequently 4 instead of 3,[1] S would tend towards 24% where both the actual and the 'natural' rates of growth would be 6%. With each interest rate and corresponding profit rate, there would be a most profitable capital output ratio and a most profitable 'natural' rate of growth, towards which the economy would tend.[2]

It is profitable for entrepreneurs to take full advantage of the growth made possible by technical progress, even in conditions of imperfect competition, because in general technical progress permits cost reduction with existing levels of output,[3] but it might not always be profitable for them to take full advantage of the growth made possible by potential economies of scale, because

[1] With the assumption (which is made here) that entrepreneurs push investment to the limit of profitable opportunity, the most profitable capital output ratio must be higher if the interest rate (and corresponding profit rate) is lower (in the absence of 'perverse' cases). The effect on the argument of inelasticity in the supply of finance and entrepreneurial inefficiency is considered below.

[2] If $t_1\%$ is the technical progress which is due to research and the replacement investment which is made when S is zero, $t_2S\%$ is further technical progress which is due to investment, and p% is the growth made possible by population increase, the 'natural' rate of growth is $(t_1+t_2.S+p)\%$. When investment is pushed to the limit of profitability, the actual rate of growth, S/C, equals the 'natural' rate, and C the actual capital output ratio is also C′ the most profitable one. Then $S/C'=t_1+t_2S+p$, $S=\frac{C'(t_1+p)}{1-t_2C'}$, and the 'natural' rate of growth is $\frac{t_1+p}{1-t_2C'}$. (NB An increase in p of 1% raises the 'natural' rate of growth by $\frac{1}{1-t_2C'}\%$ (i.e., by more than 1%), so it raises the rate of technical progress. Thus with these assumptions, faster growth of the labour force leads to faster technical progress, and faster growth of output per worker.)

[3] Some technical progress might only reduce costs with higher outputs than those currently being produced, but this possibility is neglected here.

this would require increases in output. There might then be important unexploited economies of scale in many industries producing in conditions of imperfect competition. The firms in these industries might find it impossible to lower their costs at existing levels of output, but because of potential economies of scale, they might be able to produce larger outputs at lower costs per unit and without extra workers. They would then have profitable investment opportunities whenever the demand for their products expanded. Many firms and industries might then be able to expand their outputs rapidly if they expanded simultaneously, because they would then help to create markets for each other's products by their own expansion and the consequent expansion in incomes,[1] and unexploited economies of scale would prevent the interference of diminishing returns to capital. No one firm could do this without the simultaneous expansion of other firms, because while one firm could produce a larger output at a lower cost per unit, its market would be insufficient without the expansion of other firms to allow the extra output to be sold profitably.[2]

It is possible that those commentators who believe that the mere statement of a 'target' rate of growth for the economy would allow that 'target' to be realised if the expansion of output by each industry needed to realise the 'target' was worked out and publicised, might have this kind of situation in mind. The situation is one where full employment and simultaneous profit maximisation by all entrepreneurs would not be sufficient to realise the fastest possible rate of growth compatible with profitability, and where some kind of stimulus would be needed to persuade entrepreneurs to expand more quickly than they would otherwise choose to in order to realise the 'full natural' rate of growth of the economy.

The 'natural' rate of growth could be thought of as 'the rate of advance which the increase in population and technological improvements allow when entrepreneurs maximise their profits independently', and then 'the greatest rate of advance compatible with profitability which the increase in population and technological improvements could allow' would be the 'full natural' rate of growth.

The 'full natural' rate of growth would be higher than the

[1] See Professor Allyn Young's, 'Increasing Returns and Economic Progress', *Economic Journal*, 1928.

[2] The firm would only be precluded from selling a larger output at lower prices if there were lapses from perfect competition. But this is precisely the situation likely to prevail where economies of scale are important.

'natural' rate if there were unexploited economies of scale which could only be exploited if industries expanded simultaneously. If these economies of scale were exploited, there would be an increase in the rate of growth due to this, and an additional increase because there would be a rise (which would otherwise have been unprofitable) in S, and this would raise the rate of technical progress and the highest 'natural' rate of growth which could be profitable. In these circumstances, government intervention to raise the rate of investment, or to institute planned rates of expansion by different industries, might well result in a faster rate of growth.

Difficulty in obtaining finance, entrepreneurial inefficiency, and economic growth

It has been assumed so far in the argument that the supply of finance is infinitely elastic at the ruling rate of interest, and that investment is always pushed (by individual entrepreneurs) to the limit of profitable opportunity. In fact, it has been assumed that all investments capable of earning any profit in excess of the interest cost of obtaining finance plus the risk premium entrepreneurs require are always carried out. In an actual economy there are many reasons why this might not happen, and the ways in which the rate of growth would be affected by inelasticity in the supply of finance, and entrepreneurial inefficiency will now be considered.

If the supply of finance was not infinitely elastic, some firms would be unable to take advantage of profitable investment opportunities because of difficulty in obtaining finance. The difficulty could be due to the decisions of banks and other financial institutions, or to the consequences of government policy to restrict credit. Firms might also be unable to invest as much as they wished because of difficulty in obtaining machinery without delivery delays, or because of builders' delays before factory extensions could be completed. All these factors would either have the effect of lengthening the actual life of capital[1] because of occasional delays to new investment, or of raising the notional profit rate an investment had to be expected to earn before a firm would be prepared to carry it out. The effect of a higher notional profit rate would be both that new capital with a lower capital output ratio might be preferred to new capital with a higher capital output ratio, and that the replacement of capital might be

[1] I use the term 'life of capital' to refer to the life (in years) of 'fixed' capital.

postponed because the cost of production with new capital would be raised (by the effect of the higher notional profit rate on capital cost), while the cost of production with existing capital would be almost unchanged.[1] The effect of these factors is then to lower the capital output ratio of new capital, and to increase the actual length of life of capital.[2]

There is the further possibility that while entrepreneurs might be able to afford to carry out potentially profitable investments, they might not do so because of inefficiency. Firms able to obtain finance might not invest as soon as it became profitable to do so because of ignorance, conservatism, or lack of the expertise needed to supervise the working of more complex machinery. In particular their managements might continue to use old machinery long after it had become profitable to replace it. There might also be restrictive practices in an industry which held up profitable investment. In all these cases, entrepreneurs and managements with better judgement and skill would eventually take over the markets concerned, but at any one time there would be many entrepreneurs who (for some reason or other) did not take full advantage of the profitable investment opportunities open to them.

The effect of the various kinds of entrepreneurial inefficiency outlined would be to lengthen the actual life of capital; and because inefficient or conservative entrepreneurs are likely to be biased against more complex methods of production which are also likely to be the most capitally intensive, the capital output ratio of new capital would sometimes be lower than the most profitable capital output ratio.

Thus the effects of inelasticity in the supply of finance and entrepreneurial inefficiency are likely to be a life of capital longer than the most profitable length of life, and a capital output ratio of new

[1] It would be raised very slightly because the interest cost of work in progress (including the interest cost of the wages paid in the period between the start of production and the sale of the product) would be increased.

[2] A higher notional profit rate would also give incentives to entrepreneurs to design or install new capital of a less durable kind, because it would increase the notional cost of durability. It is assumed in the argument that follows that the immediate effect of a higher notional profit rate of making new capital appear to be more expensive relative to existing capital, and so of lengthening the actual life of capital, would outweigh any effect it might have in shortening the life of capital through reductions in the durability of new capital. Thus it is assumed that on balance, difficulty in obtaining finance lengthens the actual life of capital. It would be very strange if it shortened it.

capital lower than the most profitable capital output ratio, and these would affect the rate of growth. Their effect on the rate of growth will now be shown.

The effect on the rate of growth of a longer life of capital (longer, that is, than the most profitable length of life) will be considered first. If the life of capital in an economy is longer, the proportion of workers who are equipped with old capital must be greater, and since 'output per worker' (referred to subsequently as 'labour productivity') is lower with old than with new capital, average labour productivity must be lower. Thus, where two economies are similar in every respect except that their lives of capital are different, the one with the longer life of capital will have lower average labour productivity, and therefore lower total output. It might be thought that it would also have a slower rate of growth, but this is not so. If the life of capital is fifty years in one economy and ten years in another, they would both have the same rate of growth if the rate of technical progress and the rate of population increase was the same in both, and the capital output ratio of new capital was constant.[1]

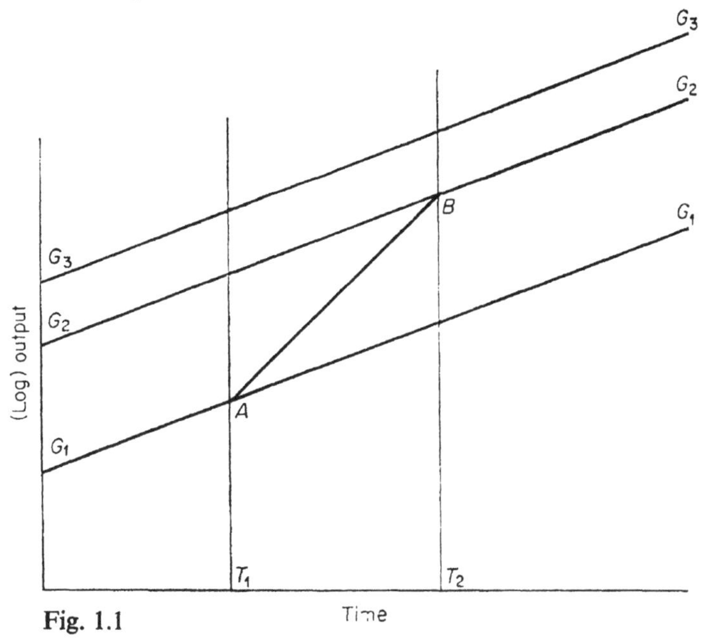

Fig. 1.1

[1] Professor Joan Robinson pointed this out in lectures she gave in Cambridge in 1956. It is proved in the Mathematical Appendix to this chapter, but non-mathematical readers might find the following argument convincing. It refers to a situation where the labour force is constant, but it could easily be

The effect of a shortening of the life of capital on the rate of growth is illustrated in figure 1.1. It is assumed that the capital output ratio of new capital is constant, so changes in labour productivity with new capital depend only on technical progress. G_1G_1 is the growth path an economy would follow if the length of life of its capital was forty years, while G_2G_2 is the growth path an economy would follow with a life of capital of twenty years. The slopes of these GG lines show what the rate of growth would be if these lives of capital were maintained, and they depend simply on technical progress and population increase, i.e., on the 'natural'

---

extended to apply to a situation where the labour force is growing. It is assumed that labour productivity with any capital is higher than with capital a year older by d% because it has been used a year less, and by t′% because it has benefited from an extra year's technical progress (i.e., 'embodied' technical progress is t′% per annum), so altogether it is (d+t′)% higher. If labour productivity with new capital is 1, and the number of workers equipped with it is p, its total output is 1.p. If p workers also work with one-year-old capital, labour productivity with it is (d+t′)% less, so its total output is $1.p.\left(1-\frac{d+t'}{100}\right)$ and if p workers work with two-year-old capital its total output is $1.p\left(1-\frac{d+t'}{100}\right)^2$, and the total output with six-year-old capital is $1.p\left(1-\frac{d+t'}{100}\right)^6$.

If the life of capital is L years, total output is:

$$1\left\{p+p\left(1-\frac{d+t'}{100}\right)+p\left(1-\frac{d+t'}{100}\right)^2+\ldots+p\left(1-\frac{d+t'}{100}\right)^{L-1}\right\}.$$

In the following year, with technical progress of t%, where t equals t′ plus t″ (where t″ is technical progress of the kind which applies to both old and new capital, or 'disembodied' technical progress), labour productivity with new capital is t% greater than in the year before, so labour productivity with it is $\left(1+\frac{t}{100}\right)$ instead of 1, but labour productivity with one-year-old capital is (d+t′)% less than this as before, and labour productivity with six-year-old capital is $\left(1-\frac{d+t'}{100}\right)^6$ times labour productivity with new capital, as before.

Total output in the following year is then:

$$\left(1+\frac{t}{100}\right)\left\{p+p\left(1-\frac{d+t'}{100}\right)+p\left(1-\frac{d+t'}{100}\right)^2+\ldots+p\left(1-\frac{d+t'}{100}\right)^{L-1}\right\},$$

which is just t% higher than the total output of the year before, since the term inside the large bracket is unchanged, and the term outside it has increased from 1 to $\left(1+\frac{t}{100}\right)$, i.e., by t%. The rate of growth of output is then (t′+t″)% or t%, when L, the life of capital, is constant.

rate of growth, and an economy which is moving along a GG line simply grows at its 'natural' rate. If the 'natural' rate of growth was the same with a life of capital of twenty years and a life of forty years, an economy growing along G_2G_2 would have the same growth rate as an economy growing along G_1G_1, and G_2G_2 would then have the same slope as G_1G_1, i.e., G_2G_2 would be parallel to G_1G_1. However, output is higher each year on G_2G_2, because the life of capital is shorter, and G_2G_2 is drawn above G_1G_1 to show this. Thus the height of a GG line shows what the output of an economy moving along it will be in different years, and its slope shows what the economy's rate of growth will be.

If the economy with growth path G_1G_1 started to invest in new capital more quickly at time T_1, the life of its capital would begin to get shorter (because it would be replaced sooner) and it would rise above G_1G_1. If its life of capital was twenty years at time T_2, it would reach G_2G_2; and it would move along G_2G_2 instead of G_1G_1 for as long as the life of its capital remained twenty years. Between times T_1 and T_2 it would move from A to B, and its growth rate would be faster than the 'natural' rate because the slope of AB is necessarily steeper than the slopes of G_1G_1 and G_2G_2. Once it reached B, its rate of growth would revert to the 'natural' rate unless its life of capital continued to shorten, in which case it would move towards a still higher growth path G_3G_3 (where the life of capital is ten years). Its rate of growth would only be higher than the 'natural' rate while it was being augmented by an actual *shortening* of the life of capital, i.e., while it was moving from one GG line to a higher one. If there was an upper limit to the share of gross investment in the National Product which was practicable (for political reasons, for instance), there would also be a limit to the extent to which the life of capital could be shortened, and when that limit was reached the economy would reach a high GG line and move along it, and then its rate of growth would simply depend on the slope of that GG line, i.e., on the 'natural' rate of growth.

In Table 1.1 in the Mathematical Appendix to this chapter, the effect of various lengths of life of capital on average labour productivity are worked out, and it is possible to work out the effect of a move from G_1G_1 to G_2G_2 on output and the rate of growth with its help. For instance, suppose labour productivity with any capital was always 5% higher than with capital which was a year older (because ageing of capital caused a fall in labour productivity of d% a year, and capital which was a year less old had benefited from 'embodied' technical progress of t'% a year, and (d+t')%=5%), then average labour productivity when capital had a forty-year life would be 43·2% of the labour productivity with new capital, and it would be 63·2% when capital had a twenty-year life; so average labour productivity would be 46·3% higher with a twenty-year life (since 63·2 is 46·3% higher than 43·2), and therefore output along G_2G_2 where the life of capital is twenty years would be 46·3% higher than output along G_1G_1 where the life of capital is forty years.

Thus, when an economy moved along AB, it would have 46·3% of growth while it moved up AB in addition to growth at the 'natural' rate. If the 'natural' rate was 3% a year, and T_1 and T_2 were twenty years apart (i.e., if it took twenty years to shorten the life of capital from forty years to twenty), there would be an extra 46·3% of growth spread over these twenty years, or an extra 2·0% a year, and the overall growth rate in this twenty-year period would be (3+2·0)% or 5%. If (d+t')% was 2% instead of 5%, G_2G_2 would only be 19·8% above G_1G_1, and the extra growth along AB would only be 19·8% spread over the twenty years, or 0·9% a year, and the overall growth rate in the twenty-year period would be 3·9% instead of 5%. Other examples can be worked out with the help of Table 1.1 in the Mathematical Appendix. Naturally enough, a smaller (d+t') always reduces the extra growth due to shortening of the life of capital.

When the life of capital is reduced, the share of gross investment in output has to be increased,[1] and so the share of consumption is reduced. The growth in consumption is consequently less than the growth in output referred to in the last paragraph. For instance, when the life of capital is reduced from forty years to twenty (and output is consequently increased 46·3%), it can be seen in Table 1.1 that the share of gross investment in output is increased from 5·8C% (where C is the gross capital output ratio of new capital) to 7·9C%, so an extra 2·1C% of output has to consist of investment, and as a result of this the growth in consumption is less than

[1] It would be wrong to suppose that halving the life of capital (when the size of the labour force is constant) would double the *share* of gross investment in the National Product. Twice as many workers would need to be equipped with new capital each year if the life of capital was halved, and if the new capital was unchanged, twice the total *amount* of gross investment would be needed, but because the National Product would be higher owing to the shorter life of capital, it would not be necessary to invest twice as great a *share* of the National Product. This was pointed out to me by Professor Peter Wiles.

46·3%. If C equalled 2 the growth in consumption would be 39·3%, if C equalled 3 it would be 35·0%, and if C equalled 4 it would be 30·1%. If the life of capital was reduced further from twenty years to ten years in a move from G_2G_2 to G_3G_3, output would rise a further 24·5%, but the further rise in consumption would only be 10·3% if C was 2, 1% if C equalled 3, and consumption would actually fall by 9·4% if C equalled 4. There would be a particular life of capital which maximised consumption (ten and a half years if C equalled 2, fourteen years if C equalled 3, and seventeen years if C equalled 4), and once this life was reached, further shortening of the life of capital would cause a reduction in consumption.[1]

It was suggested earlier that the rate of technical progress might be higher when the share of investment was higher, and if this was the case, higher GG lines would have a steeper slope than lower GG lines, and when an economy moved to a higher GG line its growth rate would be permanently higher, because its rate of technical progress would be higher when capital was replaced more frequently. A move to a higher GG line than the line where consumption is maximised might then be justifiable, because the rate of technical progress would be higher on the higher GG line, and consumption would eventually become higher on this line because of the faster rate of technical progress associated with it.

The argument can be reversed. If there was a lengthening of the life of capital because of increased entrepreneurial inefficiency, or difficulty in obtaining finance, the economy would move to a lower GG line. There would then be an abnormally low rate of growth while a *lengthening* of the life of capital occurred, but once the economy was adjusted to the longer life of capital it would move along the GG line appropriate to that length of life, and output would once again grow at the 'natural' rate. There would, of course, be a permanent reduction in the rate of growth if the longer life of capital caused a reduction in the rate of technical progress.

The same analysis can be used to illustrate how the rate of growth changes when the capital output ratio of new capital is raised.[2] Labour productivity must be higher with capital with

[1] The circumstances in which the life of capital would be such that consumption would be maximised will be considered in Chapter 6.

[2] It might be raised, either because of increased availability of finance, or because a reduction in interest and profit rates made it profitable for entrepreneurs to purchase new capital with a higher capital output ratio.

a higher capital output ratio. An economy where new capital had a higher capital output ratio (and a constant length of life of capital) would therefore move along a higher GG line than an economy with a lower capital output ratio of new capital (and the same length of life of capital). An economy would therefore be able to move to a higher GG line if the capital output ratio of its new capital was raised, and its rate of growth would be higher during the move to the higher GG line. As with the life of capital, an increase in the capital output ratio of new capital would raise the necessary share of investment, and the growth in consumption would consequently be less than the growth in gross output. As with the life of capital, if there was a connection between the share of investment and the rate of technical progress, the higher GG lines would have a steeper slope, and a higher capital output ratio would then permanently raise the rate of growth. A reduction in the capital output ratio would take the economy to a lower GG line, and result in a lower rate of growth while the reduction occurred, and also subsequently if technical progress was less.

Economies move along lower GG lines than they could move along because of inelasticity in the supply of finance and entrepreneurial ineffiicency, which lengthen the actual life of capital, and lower the capital output ratio of new capital. Their levels of output are consequently always some way below the levels which could be achieved if the supply of finance was elastic and entrepreneurs always invested when it was profitable for them to do so. Their rates of growth, on the other hand, depend on the slope of the GG lines they move along, and these depend on their 'natural' rates of growth, which in turn depend on their technical progress and population increase.[1] When entrepreneurial inefficiency, or inelasticities in the supply of finance are reduced, an economy can move to a higher GG line, and while this move is made (and it will require an increase in the share of gross investment), the economy's rate of growth will be higher than the 'natural' rate.

Conclusion

It is now possible to summarise the various ways in which the rate of growth of an economy with full employment could be raised. Fundamentally its rate of growth depends on technical progress and population increase, and any policy which resulted in a higher rate of technical progress would raise the rate of growth. An in-

[1] Cf Professor Peter Wiles's distinction between 'brakes' and 'handicaps' in *The Political Economy of Communism*, Blackwell, 1962, pp. 385–8.

crease in the rate of technical progress would steepen the GG line along which the economy was moving, and its rate of growth would consequently rise.[1] If faster technical progress took the form of a more rapid annual increase in the productivity of new capital relatively to older capital (i.e., an increase in t′), it would also become profitable to replace capital more frequently (because the cost of production with new capital would fall more rapidly relatively to the cost of production with old capital), and the economy would also move to a higher GG line. Thus the effect of a higher rate of technical progress could be both steeper GG lines, and a move to a higher GG line, so that there might be a particularly rapid rate of growth in the years immediately following an increase in the rate of technical progress.

A second and further increase in the rate of growth would be possible if there was a 'full natural' rate of growth higher than the 'natural' rate because of unexploited economies of scale in imperfectly competitive industries. Government stimulation of expansion (through stimulation of investment, and possibly through planned 'target' rates of growth for each industry) might then cause an economy to grow at its 'full natural' rate, when otherwise it would simply grow at its 'natural' rate.

The third way in which the growth rate could be raised would be through the elimination of some of the factors causing inelasticity in the supply of finance and entrepreneurial inefficiency. The elimination of restrictive practices, and changes in the tax system designed to lessen or counteract entrepreneurial inefficiency would help here.[2] Any reduction in entrepreneurial inefficiency or increase

[1] It would do this however inefficient entrepreneurs were, because the degree of entrepreneurial inefficiency in the economy is already allowed for by the fact that the economy is moving along a lower GG line than the highest possible one.

[2] The following would be a particularly helpful change in the UK which will be discussed in detail in Chapter 6. At present, firms pay a certain proportion of their profits in taxation. The result is that a firm with lower production costs than competing firms pays about 50% of the resultant extra profit to the government, while a firm with high enough costs to prevent it from earning any profit pays almost no tax. If there was no taxation of profits, and instead all the firms in the economy paid the same amount of tax, but paid it in proportion to their use of labour (through a 'pay-roll' tax), or of all resources (through a 'value-added tax'), the entire profit due to lower costs of production than competitors would go to the firm concerned, and there would be a great increase in the tax liability of firms with high costs of production. A change of this kind would place high-cost firms in a much weaker competitive position, and it would consequently speed up the rate at which efficient entrepreneurs could take over the markets of less efficient entrepreneurs.

in the availability of finance would allow an economy to move to a higher GG line through consequent shortening of the life of capital, and increases in the capital output ratio of new capital. This would temporarily increase the rate of growth, and it would increase it permanently if a larger share of investment raised the rate of technical progress. A reduction in the interest rate might also allow an economy to move to a higher GG line.

There is a fourth possibility which has not yet been discussed. If, in an economy, there was a shortage of certain kinds of skilled labour such as scientists, engineers, or managerial staff with the ability to plan and supervise complicated processes of production, industries with substantial opportunities for growth might not be able to expand, and the products concerned would often need to be imported. If the rate of technical progress was higher in these industries than in others, an economy in this position would have a lower overall rate of technical progress, and therefore a lower rate of growth. Its rate of technical progress, and so its rate of growth, would be raised if more workers of these kinds were trained, and there would probably also be a beneficial effect on its balance of payments.

An increased share of gross investment in the National Product is not needed initially to take advantage of opportunities for growth created by a steepening of the slope of the GG line along which the economy is moving, but an increased share of gross investment is needed immediately to take advantage of opportunities to move to higher GG lines. Thus an immediately increased share of gross investment would not be needed to take advantage of faster technical progress, but it would be needed to take advantage of opportunities to move to higher GG lines created by increased availability of finance, or increased entrepreneurial efficiency, and it would also be needed to take advantage of a 'full natural' rate of growth higher than the 'natural' rate.

If an opportunity for growth was created by the elimination of some of the conditions which kept the economy on a low GG line, and there was no subsequent fall in the share of consumption in the National Product, so that the share of investment could not be increased, there would be demand-induced inflationary pressure, and factors such as increased difficulty in obtaining finance (due possibly to government measures to restrict credit) and increasing delays in the time needed to obtain machinery would prevent the economy from moving to a higher GG line.

Thus an increased share of investment in the National Product is often needed to take advantage of opportunities for faster growth, but investment only creates opportunities for growth in so far as the rate of technical progress is related to the share of investment, and investment itself is unlikely to create enough technical progress to overcome diminishing returns. There is then likely to be a limit to the share of an economy's National Product which can be invested profitably when the rate of interest is given. To obtain the highest possible rate of growth when there is full employment, as much technical opportunity for growth as possible must be created, and it must then be ensured that there will be sufficient investment to allow this to be exploited.

In an economy with substantial unemployment, or under-employment of labour, the technical opportunity for growth is almost unlimited, and there is no reason to suppose that an increase in the share of investment would not raise the rate of growth in at least the same proportion. The problem of obtaining the fastest possible rate of growth is then mainly one of obtaining the largest possible share of investment.

MATHEMATICAL APPENDIX[1]

1 It is shown here that the total labour force grows at rate p when the number of workers equipped with new capital at each point in time grows at rate p, and the life of capital is constant. The number of workers available to work new capital grows at an exponential rate p, and at time n it is $k.e^{pn}$. Then the number of workers available to work new capital at time $(n-b)$ was $k.e^{p(n-b)}$. If all the workers available to work new capital are always equipped with it, and capital is worked until it is L years old, the total labour force at time n is $\int_0^L k.e^{p(n-b)}db$ which equals $k.e^{pn}\left(\frac{1-e^{-pL}}{p}\right)$. This grows at exponential rate p when k, L and p are constant.

[1] The mathematics in this Mathematical Appendix has been much influenced by the work of J. Black. See his 'Technical progress and optimum savings', *Review of Economic Studies*, 1962. For expositional convenience, p, t and d are expressed as fractions in the mathematical statements of this Appendix. For instance, where technical progress is 2% per annum, t is 0·02 and not 2%.

2 It is shown here that output grows at rate (t+p) when labour productivity with new capital equipment produced at successive points in time grows at exponential rate t, and where p, t, L and d (the rate at which labour productivity falls as capital becomes older) are all constant. Labour productivity with capital equipment produced at time n is at an annual rate of $j.e^{tn}$ when the equipment is new. Labour productivity with all equipment falls at rate d as the equipment becomes older, so at time (n+b) labour productivity with equipment produced at time n will be $j.e^{(tn-db)}$. Labour productivity with capital equipment produced at time (n−b) was $j.e^{t(n-b)}$ when it was new, and it is $j.e^{t(n-b)-db}$ at time n. $k.e^{p(n-b)}$ workers were equipped with capital which is b years old in year n, so the total output of b year old capital at time n is at an annual rate of $k.e^{p(n-b)}.j.e^{t(n-b)-db}$ which equals $j.k.e^{n(p+t.)}e^{-(p+t+d)b}$. Then total output at time n is at an annual rate of $\int_0^L j.k.e^{n(p+t)}.e^{-b(p+t+d)}db$, if capital is scrapped when it is L years old, which equals $j.k.e^{n(p+t)}\left(\frac{1-e^{-(p+t+d)L}}{p+d+t}\right)$. This grows at an exponential rate of (p+t) when j, k, p, d, t and L are constant, and the result follows *a fortiori* if p or d is zero, i.e., if the labour force is constant or if capital does not deteriorate.

3 Average labour productivity in the economy at time n is now worked out. Since the labour force at time n is $k.e^{pn}\left(\frac{1-e^{-pL}}{p}\right)$ and total output at time n is at an annual rate of $j.k.e^{(p+t)n}\left(\frac{1-e^{-(p+d+t)L}}{p+t+d}\right)$, average labour productivity at time n must be at an annual rate of

$$j.e^{tn}\,.\,\frac{p}{p+d+t}\,.\,\frac{1-e^{-(p+t+d)L}}{1-e^{-pL}}.$$

This grows at an exponential rate of t when j, p, d, t, and L are constant. If p=0, i.e., if the labour force is constant, average labour productivity is

$$j.e^{tn}\,.\,\frac{1-e^{-(p+t+d)L}}{(p+t+d)L}\ \left(\text{since } \frac{p}{1-e^{-pL}}=\frac{p}{pL-(p^2L^2)/2!\,..}\right.$$

which tends towards 1/L as p tends towards zero).

4 The share of investment in output is now worked out. If the cost of the capital needed to equip a worker is C times the annual output per worker with that capital when new (so that C is the gross capital output ratio of new capital), then since the annual rate of output of new capital at time n is $j.k.e^{(p+t)n}$, gross investment at time n is $C.j.k.e^{(p+t)n}$. Since gross output at time n is at an annual rate of

$j.k.e^{(p+t)n}\left(\frac{1-e^{-(p+t+d)L}}{p+t+d}\right)$, the share of gross investment in gross output at time n is $\frac{C(p+t+d)}{1-e^{-(p+t+d)L}}$ which is constant when C, p, d, t, and L are constant.

5 The complications due to different kinds of technical progress are now incorporated in the argument. If technical progress consists partly of 'disembodied' technical progress, or improvements which result in increases in labour productivity with all capital (so that this increases at rate t''), and partly of 'embodied' technical progress, or improvements which result in increases in labour productivity which are confined to new capital (labour productivity with new capital rises at rate t, but since labour productivity with old capital rises at rate t'', the increase in labour productivity involving new capital alone is at rate $(t-t'')$ which equals t'), the argument is affected in the following ways. First $(t'+t'')$ can be substituted for t, and secondly $(d-t'')$ can be substituted for d, since labour productivity with old capital falls at rate d because of deterioration with use, and rises at rate t'' because of technical progress which affects all capital. Substituting these, it can be seen that total output at time n is $j.k.e^{(p+t'+t'')n}\left(\frac{1-e^{-(p+t'+d)L}}{p+d+t'}\right)$, average labour productivity at time n is $j.e^{(t'+t'')n}\cdot\frac{p}{p+t'+d}\cdot\frac{1-e^{-(p+t'+d)L}}{p+t'+d}$, and the share of gross investment at time n is $\frac{C(p+t'+d)}{1-e^{-(p+t'+d)L}}$, which is less than the share of gross investment in paragraph 4 since t' is less than t. The effect of the change is to leave the growth rate unaltered, but to raise average labour productivity, and to reduce the share of investment.

6 Table 1.1 is worked out to show the effect of the rate of technical progress, the rate of deterioration of capital, and the life of capital on average labour productivity (which is given in this table as the percentage of average labour productivity to labour productivity with new capital), and the percentage share of investment.

TABLE 1.1

L		Constant population (p=0) d+t′						(d+t′) = 4% p			
		1%	2%	3%	4%	5%	10%	0%	1%	2%	3%
5	Average labour productivity	97·6	95·2	92·9	90·6	88·5	78·7	90·6	90·7	90·8	90·8
	Share of investment	20·5C	21·0C	21·5C	22·1C	22·6C	25·4C	22·1C	22·6C	23·1C	23·7C
10	Average labour productivity	95·2	90·6	86·4	82·4	78·7	63·2	82·4	82·7	83·0	83·2
	Share of investment	10·5C	11·0C	11·6C	12·1C	12·7C	15·8C	12·1C	12·7C	13·3C	13·9C
20	Average labour productivity	90·6	82·4	75·2	68·8	63·2	43·2	68·8	69·7	70·7	71·6
	Share of investment	5·5C	6·1C	6·7C	7·3C	7·9C	11·6C	7·3C	7·9C	8·6C	9·3C
30	Average labour productivity	86·4	75·2	65·9	58·2	51·8	31·7	58·2	59·9	61·7	63·4
	Share of investment	3·9C	4·4C	5·1C	5·7C	6·4C	10·5C	5·7C	6·4C	7·2C	8·0C
40	Average labour productivity	82·4	68·8	58·2	49·9	43·2	24·5	49·9	52·5	55·0	57·6
	Share of investment	3·0C	3·6C	4·3C	5·0C	5·8C	10·2C	5·0C	5·8C	6·6C	7·4C

2

RESEARCH AND TECHNICAL PROGRESS

Introduction

Technical progress is perhaps the most important of the factors which make economic growth possible. Technical progress and population increase together determine the 'natural' rate of growth, and the argument of Chapter 1 suggested that this is likely to have an important influence on actual growth rates. In this chapter, some of the factors which may contribute to technical progress are considered. If an economy's rate of technical progress could be raised, its 'natural' rate of growth (and the slope of GG lines) would be increased, and this would have an important effect on its growth rate.

Two kinds of technical progress, t' and t'' were distinguished in Chapter 1, and the effects of both were analysed. t' or 'embodied' technical progress was technical progress which could not be exploited without new capital, and it therefore required investment. If investment was sufficient to keep the life of capital constant, the rate of growth of productive capacity due to it was $t'\%$ per annum. t'' or 'disembodied' technical progress was the technical progress which could be exploited without new capital, and this raised productive capacity by $t''\%$ per annum, whatever the rate of investment. The overall rate of technical progress, and the 'natural' rate of growth of output per worker was $(t'+t'')\%$ per annum. The factors which may contribute to 'embodied' and 'disembodied' technical progress will now be considered.

Factors which may contribute to 'embodied' technical progress

A great many factors affect the rate of technical progress. Of these, many are likely to be sociological, because education, technical mindedness, and willingness to accept change probably influence technical progress. Little can be said with certainty about factors like these in an economic argument,[1] beyond generalisations such as that a country where only a small proportion of the population receives much education, where education is biased against the sciences, where nonconformity to accepted ways of thought is discouraged, or where change can be successfully obstructed may have less technical progress than other countries.

It might be thought that random events would also have a significant effect because many inventions with important economic applications might be due to chance, or the work of particular individuals. Such events might be much less important than they appear at first sight because an immense amount of money and time is often needed before an idea with important economic applications can be used successfully, and it might well be willingness to spend money on the economic applications of ideas (where the return would often be distant and uncertain) which is most important.

Industrial research and development must make a considerable contribution to t', both because it is needed before most inventions can be exploited, and because many inventions originate from the research departments of firms. Some of the factors which influence the incentives firms have to spend money on research and development are considered below, and they must have a marked effect on the rate of 'embodied' technical progress. Sociological and random factors will also affect the rate of 'embodied' technical progress, but given two economies with the same social structure, the same educational system, and equally inventive populations, the one where more was spent on research and development would be likely to have faster 'embodied' technical progress; so the factors which cause money to be spent on research and development may be among the main *economic* factors which contribute to it.

The incentive to spend money on research and development is likely to depend on many things, of which the amount of competitive pressure to which firms are subject, and the size and security of their markets might be among the more important. Whether competition or monopoly is more likely to stimulate research has long been a matter of controversy, and a comparison will be made of the relative incentives to spend money on research

[1] See, however, E. F. Denison, *The Sources of Economic Growth in the United States and the Alternatives Before Us*, New York, Committee for Economic Development, 1962, where the contribution of education and many other factors to past US growth rates is estimated on the assumption that all factors of production were paid their marginal products.

and development to a monopoly, a firm with few competitors (i.e., an oligopoly), and a firm with a large number of competitors and therefore a very small share of the total market for its products.

The incentives to a monopoly are considered first. It might be thought that a monopoly would have little incentive to spend much on research and development because of lack of competitive pressure. Without competitive pressure, the financial and psychological pressure to reduce costs of production might appear to be slight, so that a monopoly would be under little pressure to spend much on research into superior methods of production. This is substantially true, but while a monopoly might not be under obtrusive competitive pressure, latent competitive pressure would nonetheless be present, since it would always be possible for other firms to start manufacturing the products concerned, particularly if they made technical advances the monopoly failed to make; and the monopoly's product might always be superseded through rapid technical advances in industries making products which filled a similar need.[1]

Apart from the pressure of latent competition, there are reasons why a monopoly might have incentives to spend a great deal on research and development, and it would often be able to finance this much more easily than firms which faced more competition. It would be better able to take a long view when the return from money spent on research and development could only be expected to materialise after a long interval. Most important of all, it would stand to gain more than most firms from reductions in its production costs, because the increase in profits these would permit depends largely on the number of units sold. A firm selling 1,000,000 units a year would gain at least an initial £1,000,000 a year from a cost reduction of £1 a unit, while a firm selling 10,000 units would gain at least £10,000 a year, and, in a given market, a monopolist would clearly be able to sell the largest number of units.[2] On the other hand, when firms discover new ways of reducing their costs, they can also increase their profits by taking over

[1] See Schumpeter's *Capitalism, Socialism and Democracy*, Allen and Unwin, 1943, Chapters 7 and 8. The monopolistically controlled U S bottling industry has, for instance, lost a large part of its market to the competitive industry which makes tin cans.

[2] The effect on a firm's profits of an improvement in the quality of one of its products is similar to the effect of cost reduction, because the firm can sell the improved product at a higher price, and so obtain a greater profit per unit in both cases. When the term cost reduction is used here and below, it refers to both cost reduction and product improvement.

part of their competitors' markets, and a monopoly can make much slighter gains of this kind than firms producing in competitive market situations. The main considerations, then, which suggest that a monopoly might spend a substantial amount on research and development are that it would be likely to have a secure market and the finance needed for a large research department, while the high profits obtainable from cost reduction on a large output would stimulate it to have one. On the other hand, because of lack of competitive pressure, a monopoly might not take full advantage of the opportunities open to it, and this might be a particular danger with nationalised industries which are given statutory monopoly power.

Most oligopolies also produce substantial outputs, have secure markets, and are large enough to afford adequate research departments, so they would appear to have the same incentives to spend substantial amounts on research and development as a monopoly. Their incentive is, however, not quite the same. If four firms shared a market of 1,000,000 units a year, each producing 250,000, they would each only gain an initial £250,000 a year *on their original outputs* from a cost reduction of £1 a unit, while a monopoly would gain £1,000,000 a year; so an oligopoly would apparently gain less than a monopoly from cost reduction. However, further gains are open to an oligopoly, because if one firm discovered a method of reducing costs before the other three, it would be able to take over a large part of their markets with consequent gains in both profits and future security, while a firm would be driven out of business if it persistently reduced costs more slowly than its competitors. An oligopoly might consequently expect to gain as much as a monopoly from cost reduction, and it would lose much more if it was slow to reduce costs. It might then spend as much on research and development as a monopoly producing four times as much, and it might well spend more if (as is often supposed), the fear of loss and bankruptcy is a more powerful economic stimulus than the hope of earning exceptional profits. There would moreover be four research departments in the oligopolistic industry, and each might be as large as the monopoly's single research department. Much of the work done in the four departments might be duplicated, so it would not necessarily follow that more discoveries would be made in the oligopolistic industry, but more people might be employed there on research.[1]

[1] See J. K. Galbraith's, *American Capitalism*, Hamish Hamilton, 1957.

In a highly competitive market where, for instance, a hundred firms shared a total output of 1,000,000 units a year so that each produced 10,000 units, the incentive to individual firms to have large research and development departments might well be slight. They would each only stand to gain an initial £10,000 a year from cost reductions of £1 a unit on their original outputs, and even if they could increase their outputs by as much as 1,000% at the expense of competitors, they would still only gain about £110,000 altogether, while an oligopoly would gain £250,000 on its original output alone. It does not follow from this that less research would be done altogether by the hundred firms. While each firm would have only a small incentive to spend money on research and development and therefore only a small research department, there might be a hundred such departments, and these together might employ as much staff as the larger research departments of monopolies and oligopolies; but the duplication of research would then be immense. There are, moreover, reasons why small firms would be likely to spend little on research. There are often economies of scale in research because expensive equipment and a large staff (which would be underutilised in a small department) are needed for efficient research, and small firms might be dissuaded from having research departments where this was the case, or alternatively their research departments might be underequipped and understaffed. Many small firms might also not have research departments because these could only be expected to produce results in the distant future, and small firms often need to concentrate their finance on projects likely to result in immediate profit, leaving research to firms which can afford to take a long-term view. Small firms might also be reluctant to spend much on research because the probability of making a discovery ahead of competitors might be low in an industry with a hundred firms, and entrepreneurs might think it unwise to spend money where the chance of *any* return on it was low. Thus small firms might spend little on research because the research departments they could afford would be understaffed and underequipped, because they would often only yield results in the distant future, and because there would only be a slight chance that they could achieve results ahead of competitors.

The incentives to spend money on research and development are likely to be weakened in markets where there are restrictive practices. This is because restrictive practices would more probably than not result in higher prices (because the agreements would be largely pointless unless this was the case) and the number of firms producing for a particular market would then be increased since higher prices would allow high cost producers to remain in business. The outputs of the low cost producers which could survive with lower prices would then be reduced, and the inducement to them to spend on research and development would be weakened because this depends partly on the size of a firm's output. At the same time, the incentives to spend money on research and development due to competition (i.e., the possibility of taking over competitors' markets, and the fear that competitors might do likewise) would also be weakened. The worst of both worlds is then combined where there are restrictive practices which result in higher prices, because there is neither the stimulus to research due to the monopoly's or oligopoly's high output, nor the stimulus of competition.

It is not clear from this analysis whether monopoly or oligopoly is more likely to lead to successful research and development, but it appears that there is likely to be less expenditure on research where firms have small market shares than with either monopoly or oligopoly,[1] and the incentive to spend money on research and development is likely to be particularly weakened where there are restrictive practices.

It is not *certain* that government intervention prompting monopolies or oligopolies to spend more than they would choose to on research and development would raise the rate of growth. If monopolies and oligopolies always pushed their expenditure on research and development to the limit of profitability, they would spend up to the point where the expected yield from research and development expenditure was just equal to the cost of finance (where this included a factor allowing for risk); so investment in research would be expected to yield the same amount at the margin as investment in capital equipment. Then both kinds of investment might have the same marginal capital output ratio, and marginal expenditures on each might then make the same contribution to growth.[2] Any government stimulation of research at the expense of investment in fixed capital might then reduce the rate of growth. Of course, expenditures on research and on fixed capital could

[1] It is interesting that in 1938 one-third of all research workers in the U S worked for only thirteen companies (J. Steindl, *Small and Big Business*, Blackwell, 1945, p. 17).

[2] See n. 1, p. 17.

only conceivably make the same marginal contribution to growth if research expenditure was pushed towards the limit of profitability to the same extent as investment in fixed capital, and one important reason why this might not happen is because monopolies or oligopolies might not be subject to enough competitive pressure to cause them to push research expenditure to the limit of profitability. It would then be important that Monopolies Commissions should frequently investigate the technical record of monopolies, and much could be made of comparisons between the technical advances they made, and those made in other countries. It would also be important to end restrictive practices which held up research and technical advance in oligopolistic industries.

It is unlikely that private entrepreneurs would push research expenditure to the point where it had the same marginal yield as investment in fixed capital where many small firms produce for a market, both because the research departments they could afford would often be too small to be effective, and because they would be likely to use a high notional cost of finance for research expenditure, which would preclude rational comparisons between the benefits from research and investment in fixed capital. Government stimulation of research and development in such industries would quite probably then raise the rate of growth because the industries themselves would not normally exploit all the profitable opportunities open to them.

The government could stimulate co-operative research in such industries, or it could itself set up and finance large research departments. This might have particularly beneficial effects in the industries which produce machinery where firms are generally small. In the U K machine tool industry, for instance,[1] 1,750 people were employed on research and development in 123 different firms between 1948 and 1957.[2] The research departments in this industry are small because each firm has only a small incentive to spend much on research and development for the reasons outlined above. A large research department set up and financed by the government might well lead to more rapid improvements in the design and development of new kinds of machinery which would

[1] Machine tools are the kind of machinery used to cut or otherwise work metal, and a large proportion of the U K's National Product consists of metal goods made with the help of machine tools.

[2] *Research and Development in the Machine Tool Industry*, Machine Tool Trades Association, 1958.

lead to faster 'embodied' technical progress.[1] The same could be said of other industries where firms are small, though more research in the industries which actually make machinery would be particularly helpful to 'embodied' technical progress, because it would lead to cost reductions wherever the machinery was used.[2]

'Embodied' technical progress might also be slower than it could be in a country where scientists and engineers were scarce and therefore expensive, and the cost of research consequently high.

In conclusion, 'embodied' technical progress can be stimulated through stimulation of research in industries where firms are small, through anti-monopoly policy which encourages monopolies to make technical advances comparable to those made abroad, through effective policy to limit restrictive practices, and through educational policy which ensures that scientists and engineers are not scarce and expensive.

Factors which may contribute to 'disembodied' technical progress

There is little that can be said about the factors which would be likely to stimulate 'disembodied' technical progress. A large part of 'disembodied' technical progress is likely to be due to newly discovered ways of rearranging or modifying capital equipment, thus raising the labour productivity of those working with it. Such improvements might be discovered and implemented by workers or managements, and it is clearly important that they should be adequately rewarded.

It is also important that workers should be confident that increases in labour productivity are in their interests, and prolonged periods of full employment together with effective guarantees that increases in productivity would not result in proportionate reductions in piece-rate payments would probably help to give them this confidence. It is not always realised that unemployment, inadequate compensation for redundancy, and downward manipulation of piece-rates when labour productivity rises may all reduce the rate of growth by causing workers to believe that increases in labour productivity would be contrary to their interests. If they

[1] It is interesting that in 1957 in the USSR, 2,450 people were employed in one organisation, ENIMS, which worked on the design and development of new machine tools. See P. E. Ward, 'How good are Soviet Engineers?', *Engineering*, 13.9.1957.

[2] See my 'Capital cost and the choice of technique', *Bulletin of the Oxford University Institute of Economics and Statistics*, 1963.

believed this, 'embodied' technical progress might also be slowed down, because workers might resist the installation of new machinery, or work it inefficiently after it was installed to prevent productivity from rising too much.

It is also important that managerial staff should have adequate skill and technical knowledge to take advantage of possible improvements to machinery, and that they should be aware of improvements made in other countries. Reports like those of the Anglo-American Productivity Council in the UK can clearly be of great help here.

Conclusion

An economy would have less 'embodied' technical progress than it could if its industries where firms are small did little research, if monopolies did not push their research and development expenditure to the limit of profitability, if there were restrictive practices which reduced the profitability of technical advance, and if scientists and engineers were scarce and expensive, or general education was inadequate.

It would have less 'disembodied' technical progress if many workers believed that increases in labour productivity were contrary to their interests, if managerial personnel were insufficiently skilled to modify and improve machinery, and if they were ignorant of improvements made in other firms and economies.

APPENDIX

The 'neutrality' of technical progress

Technical progress can be thought of as 'neutral' if the capital output ratio of the new capital it is most profitable to use remains unchanged, when the rate of profit is unchanged.[1] Then technical progress is 'capital using' if the most profitable capital output ratio rises as a result of technical advance, and 'capital saving' if it falls. An example of 'capital using' technical progress might be the development of certain kinds of capital equipment for 'automation' which have a higher capital output

[1] This definition is similar to Sir Roy Harrod's definition of a 'neutral' advance as 'one which, at a constant rate of interest, does not disturb the value of the capital coefficient' (*Towards a Dynamic Economics*, p. 23).

ratio than non-automatic equipment, and at the same time permit production at lower cost. The rapid progress of road relative to rail transport may be an example of 'capital saving' technical progress, because the capital required relatively to output is usually less for road transport.

A distinction is sometimes made between 'capital saving' and 'labour saving' technical progress, but this distinction is less clear than that between 'capital saving' and 'capital using' technical progress. Technical progress which permits a rise in labour productivity is 'labour saving' (since it reduces the labour needed to produce a unit of output) and there is little technical progress which is not 'labour saving', because a technical advance rarely makes it profitable to adopt a new method of production with *lower* labour productivity. In fact, non 'labour saving' technical progress (i.e., technical progress which makes it profitable to *reduce* labour productivity) is almost an 'empty box', and almost all technical progress is 'labour saving'. But much of the 'labour saving' technical progress is also 'capital saving' in that it permits a reduction in the capital output ratio as well as a rise in labour productivity. Then 'labour saving' and 'capital saving' technical progress are not distinct. The distinction between 'capital saving' and 'capital using' technical progress is, in contrast, quite clear, and there is much technical progress of both kinds.

A rise in the actual capital output ratio in an economy would not necessarily signify that technical progress had been 'capital using'. Both 'non-neutral' technical progress *and changes in the rate of profit* can cause changes in the capital output ratio, and a rise in the actual capital output ratio could be caused by a fall in the rate of profit, while technical progress was 'neutral' or even 'capital saving'. It is only when the rate of profit is constant that it can be said with reasonable certainty that actual rises in the capital output ratio signify that technical progress was 'capital using', and falls that it was 'capital saving'.[1]

[1] Even then, it cannot be said with absolute certainty that the change in the capital output ratio was due to a bias in technical progress. If different sectors of an economy have different capital output ratios, it is possible for the average capital output ratio to rise when the capital output ratio of every sector falls, if the sectors with high capital output ratios grow relatively to the others. Then an economy's average capital output ratio could rise in a situation where the rate of profit rose, and technical progress was 'capital saving'.

3

CAPITAL INTENSITY AND ECONOMIC GROWTH

Introduction

Up to now, it has been argued that an economy's potential growth rate will depend largely on its rate of technical progress, and that this will depend mainly on its own technical discoveries. This argument may have made it appear unduly difficult for many economies to grow rapidly, since the possibility that countries can exploit technical discoveries made abroad, once patent protection ceases, has been ignored. A country's rate of technical progress will depend both on its own technical discoveries, and to a certain extent on technical advances made abroad. The exploitation of technical advances made in the U S might be particularly important to many developed economies. Labour productivity is 100% or more higher in the U S than in any other developed economy; so other developed economies could increase their outputs 100% or more if they could duplicate U S production methods, and this would allow them to maintain very rapid growth for a considerable time. Thus, in the next twenty or thirty years, many countries' potential growth rates might depend as much on the speed with which they could duplicate U S production methods as on their own technical discoveries. The duplication of U S production methods would require a great deal of investment, because capital per worker is two or three times as high in the U S as in other developed economies, but if they could be duplicated, growth rates would depend on the amounts invested, because the use of U S production methods would postpone the onset of diminishing returns to capital until productivity had been raised 100% or more.

Consequently, in the first part of this chapter, the problem of why U S entrepreneurs use techniques of production so superior to those used elsewhere will be considered. If this question could be answered, it might be possible to create conditions in Western Europe (and particularly in the UK) where entrepreneurs would wish to use US techniques, and it would then be possible for Western European economies to obtain 100% or more growth by duplicating those methods—if they invested enough. If, for instance, it was known that the use of superior US techniques of production could be attributed to the size of the US home market, other countries could obtain similar advantages by forming Customs Unions like the European Common Market. If it was known that the use of superior US techniques could be attributed to the high wage there, other countries might be able to raise the cost of labour to their entrepreneurs by raising a large proportion of their revenue through 'pay-roll' taxes. In view of the ease with which the techniques of production used in other countries can be copied, it appears plausible that some factor may be present in the US economy which allows techniques with very high labour productivity to be used there which would not be profitable elsewhere. This points to the high wage in the US, or the size of the US home market (or both together), as likely explanations.

The effect of the *real* wage (i.e., the quantity of consumer goods a worker can buy with his wage) on the technique of production and on capital intensity will be analysed below. Both real wages and labour productivity have been very much higher in the US than elsewhere for well over a hundred years, so superior labour productivity in the US is sometimes attributed to the higher US real wage.[1]

The problem which will be considered in the second part of the chapter is how countries could obtain growth through increased investment and capital intensity in addition to the growth made possible by technical progress (where this includes technical discoveries made abroad). It is often possible to raise labour productivity by substituting capital for labour in ways which are already known, though this will normally involve diminishing returns to capital. In Chapter 1, it was argued that capital per worker and labour productivity would normally be higher when the interest rate (and corresponding profit rate) was lower. The effect of interest and profit rates on the technique of production will be analysed in much more detail in the second part of this

[1] See particularly, E. Rothbarth, 'Causes of the superior efficiency of USA industry as compared with British Industry', *Economic Journal*, 1946; and Professor H. J. Habakkuk, *American and British Technology in the 19th Century*, Cambridge University Press, 1962.

chapter. It will then be possible to see more clearly how a lower profit rate could permit faster growth.

Thus, two ways in which an economy's growth rate could be raised through increased investment and capital intensity will be considered. First, by adopting US techniques of production, a Western European economy like the UK could move to the US GG line 100% or more above its own GG line, and grow at an exceptional rate while it did so without diminishing returns to capital. Second, if the profit rate in an economy became lower, it could move to the higher GG line appropriate to that profit rate, but here faster growth would not be obtained without diminishing returns to capital. In both cases, growth might become permanently faster, because technical progress might be faster on the higher GG lines when they were reached.

Real wages and capital intensity in the UK and the USA

At the start of the argument, it will be assumed that there are no tariffs or transport costs in the world. It will also be assumed that a particular capital good would have the same physical output in any country. These assumptions will be relaxed later in the argument. Complications due to the effect of the rate of profit on the relative prices of capital and consumer goods will be neglected throughout this section of the chapter.

It follows from these assumptions that a particular capital good must cost the same amount in every country (when its cost is converted into £s at current exchange rates). If a capital good costs £1,000 in the UK, it must also cost £1,000 in the US (when its $ price is converted into £s). If it cost £1,100 in the US, a profit of £100 could be made by buying it for £1,000 in the UK and selling it for £1,100 in the US, while if it cost £900 in the US, it would be profitable to buy it there and sell it in the UK for £1,000. Profitable 'arbitrage' of this kind would make its price the same in every country. Similarly, its annual product must sell for the same amount in every country. If the capital good's annual product sold for £500 in London, it could not sell for £450 or £550 in the US without similar opportunities for profitable arbitrage. Hence, if the capital good cost £1,000 in the UK, and its annual product sold for £500 there, it would necessarily cost £1,000 in any other country, and its annual product would sell for £500 in any other country. This has an important consequence. The capital good costs £1,000 in the UK, and its annual product sells there for £500, so its capital output ratio is £1,000 : £500 or

2 : 1 in the UK. Since it would also cost £1,000 and produce £500 annually in the US, its capital output ratio would also be 2 : 1 in the US—and in every other country in the world. Thus, with the assumptions of free trade, zero transport costs, and equal physical outputs from particular capital goods in every country in the world, the capital output ratios of particular capital goods would be the same throughout the world, and so would their cost (converted into £s) and the value of their annual products. This is simply an application of the law of comparative costs to capital goods and their products.

The profitability of two capital goods, A and C, in countries where real wages are different[1] is compared in Table 3.1. Their cost, their net outputs, and the wage are all expressed in £s; but the currency they are quoted in is immaterial to the argument, since any currency can be converted into any other currency at ruling exchange rates. It is assumed that both capital goods are worked by one worker. A costs £12,800 and produces net output which sells for £3,200, and its capital : output ratio is therefore 4 : 1 when it is new. C also has a capital : output ratio of 4 : 1,[2] but it costs £6,400, half as much as A, and it produces net output which sells for £1,600. Since the capital used in the US economy appears to have had about the same capital output ratio as the capital used in the UK during much of the past century,[3] while

[1] The money wages ruling in different countries converted into £s at ruling exchange rates approximate to relative real wages, because it follows from the assumption of free trade that all moveable goods must have the same price (when converted into £s) in every country in the world, and so money wages (when converted into £s) can purchase the same goods in any country. Services would, however, be cheaper in countries where the wage was lower, and given money wages would therefore purchase more services in low wage countries than in high wage countries (and more housing which is also untransportable), and real wages would therefore be somewhat higher in low wage countries than money wages (converted into £s) would indicate. This is neglected in the analysis that follows.

[2] Since its capital value will be almost zero, and its output positive when it is scrapped, its capital output ratio will then be almost zero. Its capital output ratio on average in its life might then be about 2 : 1, since it drops from 4 : 1 to a little above zero; or somewhat more than 2 : 1 if the earlier years where output is greater have more 'weight'.

[3] According to figures based on estimates by Kuznets (quoted by Professor W. Fellner in *Monetary Policies and Full Employment*, California, 1947, p. 80), the capital output ratio in the US rose from 2·58 in 1879–88 to 3·27 in 1909–18, dropped to 2·87 in 1919–28, and rose again to 3·31 in 1929–38. In the UK according to K. Maywald, 'Fire Insurance and the Capital Coefficient in Great Britain 1866–1952', *Economic History Review*, 1956, p. 102, it was

labour productivity with it has, on average, been about twice as great,[1] the choice between A and C might correspond approximately to the choice between U S and U K machinery.

TABLE 3.1

Wage W	Capital cost per worker K	Net output per worker Q	Profit per worker P=Q–W	Rate of profit[2] $r=\frac{P}{K}$
£100	A £12,800 C £6,400	£3,200 £1,600	£3,100 £1,500	24·2% 23·4%
£900	A £12,800 C £6,400	£3,200 £1,600	£2,300 £700	18·0% 10·9%
£1,800	A £12,800 C £6,400	£3,200 £1,600	£1,400 –£200	10·9% Loss

The conclusion which emerges from Table 3.1 is that a higher rate of profit is earned with A than with C, whether the wage is £1,800, £900 or £100.[3] The reason for this is simply that A and C have the same capital output ratio, and wherever two capital goods have the same capital output ratio, the one with which labour productivity is higher must always be the more profitable of the two. Capital cost per unit of output will be the same with both (because capital per unit of output is the same), but labour cost per unit of output must be less with the capital good with which labour productivity is higher.

around 3·3 in the period 1880–1914, 1·92 in 1920 and 3·0 in the period 1930–8. These sources are those quoted by Professor N. Kaldor in 'A model of economic growth', p. 592.

[1] L. Rostas, *Comparative Productivity in British and American Industry*, Cambridge University Press, 1948.

[2] If depreciation is so adjusted that the same rate of profit is earned on the net value of capital throughout its life, P/K will be the rate of profit earned throughout the life of the capital good concerned. Otherwise it will simply be the rate of profit in the first year in which the capital good is used.

[3] It is also higher if the wage is W. Then the rate of profit with A is (£3,200 – W)/£12,800, and with C it is (£1,600 – W)/£6,400. The rate of profit with A minus the rate of profit with C is then W/£12,800.

While A is always more profitable than C at any particular wage, the difference between the rates of profit with A and C varies a great deal. Where the real wage is £100 (India?), a profit rate of 24·2% is earned with A and 23·4% is earned with C, so it clearly matters little which is used. However, where the real wage is £900 (UK?), 18·0% is earned with A and 10·9% with C, and an entrepreneur using A is at a distinct advantage, and where the real wage is £1,800 (US?) the use of C is out of the question, and only entrepreneurs using A can make a profit. The effect of a higher real wage is not then to make A more profitable than C which it is in any case, but to raise the penalty for a mistaken decision to use C, which is negligible where real wages are low, and immense where they are high.[1]

In Table 3.2 the assumption that there are no tariffs and transport costs is relaxed. It is assumed that A is produced in the high wage country where the wage is £1,800 (US?), and that the country where the wage is £900 (UK?) has a tariff against the importation of A to protect its own capital goods industries, amounting with transport costs to 30%. The cost of A is then raised 30% in that country (from £12,800 to £16,640), and its net output is reduced (from £3,200 to £2,816)[2] because depreciation is raised by the higher capital cost. A's capital output ratio will then remain 4 : 1 in the high wage country where it is manufactured, but it will become £16,640 : £2,816 or 5·9 : 1 in the country with the tariff.

TABLE 3.2

W	K	Q	P	r
£900	A £16,640 C £6,400	£2,816 £1,600	£1,916 £700	11·5% 10·9%
£1,800	A £12,800 C £6,400	£3,200 £1,600	£1,400 −£200	10·9% Loss

[1] It is interesting that this point is emphasised by Professor Habakkuk (op. cit., pp. 48–52) who argues that the pressure on US entrepreneurs to use efficient methods of production was great in the nineteenth century because of the high real wage there.

[2] It is assumed (quite arbitrarily) that 10% of the extra capital cost of £3,840 has to be added to the first year's depreciation, with the result that A's net output is reduced by £384 from £3,200 to £2,816.

In the country where the wage is £900, A's margin of extra profitability is almost completely wiped out by the tariff. Without the tariff, 18·0% was earned with A and 10·9% with C. With the tariff against A, 11·5% is earned with A and 10·9% with C.

In Table 3.3 it is assumed that there are no tariffs against A in the low wage country, but that the high wage country where A is manufactured has tariffs against the importation of most manufactured products. As a result of these, both A and C and their products cost 30% more there (in £s) than in the rest of the world.[1] Its wage is also raised 30%.

TABLE 3.3

W	K	Q	P	r
£900	A £16,640 C £6,400	£2,816 £1,600	£1,916 £700	11·5% 10·9%
£2,340	A £16,640 C £8,320	£4,160 £2,080	£1,820 −£260	10·9% Loss

The result is exactly the same as in Table 3.2. Because the cost of A is raised 30% to entrepreneurs in other countries who wish to use it, its capital output ratio is raised from 4 : 1 to 5·9 : 1, and its margin of extra profitability is reduced to exactly the same extent as it is where the importing countries themselves impose a tariff.

In Table 3.4 there are no tariffs and transport costs, but A produces 30% less net output when it is used in countries other than the high wage country where it is manufactured. This may be because special skills are needed to work it effectively, and only entrepreneurs or workers in the high wage country possess these, or it may be because a larger market is needed to permit it to be worked at full capacity, and the market of the high wage country is larger than those of other countries. The effect is that its net output in other countries is 30% less than £3,200, i.e., £2,240, and its capital output ratio in other countries is therefore £12,800 : £2,240, or 5·7 : 1.

[1] It would only be possible for the price of both A and its product to be higher if the high wage country was a net importer of A's product, but this was the U S's position with regard to many manufactured goods in the nineteenth century.

TABLE 3.4

W	K	Q	P	r
£900	A £12,800 C £6,400	£2,240 £1,600	£1,340 £700	10·5% 10·9%
£1,800	A £12,800 C £6,400	£3,200 £1,600	£1,400 −£200	10·9% Loss

Here A's margin of extra profitability over C is more than eliminated in the country where the wage is £900, when it produces 30% less in that country than it produces in the high wage country.

It is now possible to suggest an explanation for the higher labour productivity in the U S economy. There is no evidence that the capital used by U S entrepreneurs has generally had higher capital output ratios than the capital used in the U K, while labour productivity has been higher in the U S for some time. It therefore seems likely that capital goods such as A have been designed and used in the U S, while capital goods such as C have been designed and used in the U K. That the capital goods industries in the U S have been able to design and produce capital goods which have been unambiguously superior (i.e., superior at any wage) to those designed and produced in the U K must be the fundamental reason for U S superiority. Disregarding tariffs, transport costs, and the differing efficiencies of labour and managements, U S capital goods would have been much more profitable in the U K than the capital goods actually used. In Table 3.1 the rate of profit with A is 18%, and it is 10·9% with C in the country where the wage is £900; and if a few entrepreneurs had used A, they would gradually have forced entrepreneurs to stop using C, in spite of imperfections in competition, because their potential cost advantage would have been considerable.[1]

On the other hand, a tariff of 30% (together with transport costs) against A, or tariffs in the country which produces A which makes its price level 30% higher, or inefficient working of A which

[1] In Table 3.1 where the capital output ratio of A and C is 4 : 1, a rate of profit which is 7·1% higher can be earned with A, but alternatively the same rate of profit could be earned, and a price which is 4 × 7·1% or 28·4% lower could be charged.

causes it to produce 30% less would each have been sufficient to make its advantage over C negligible (or to wipe it out altogether) in the examples considered.

Thus the secondary cause of higher U S labour productivity (the primary cause being the design of superior capital goods in the U S) is that one or more of these factors prevent (and have prevented) the profitable use of U S capital goods in the U K. In the nineteenth century, U S tariffs were substantial and the U S was a substantial net importer of manufactured goods, so the prices of many manufactured goods were higher in the U S than in the U K, a position analagous to that in Table 3.3. Since 1932, the U K has had a tariff against foreign machinery, currently of 20% (and 30% with an 'import surcharge' of 10%), and this together with transport costs would make A about 30% more expensive in the U K than in the U S, a position analogous to that in Table 3.2. The U K tariff may then be almost sufficient to wipe out A's advantage, and in consequence most of the U S capital goods the U K imports may well be among those which are superior to A, i.e., those where labour productivity is more than twice as great as that with U K produced capital goods. If U K labour and managements operate U S machinery less efficiently than U K machinery, or if the U K market is too small to allow U S machinery to be worked to capacity, there would be additional reasons why U S machinery (with productivity 100% higher on average with it than with U K produced machinery) is not more used in the U K, but in the examples in Tables 3.2–3.3 tariffs are a sufficient explanation.

If U S machinery is unambiguously superior to U K machinery but the U K is prevented from making use of it because of tariffs and transport costs, it is still necessary to explain why machinery such as A is not manufactured in the U K, since its design cannot be kept secret for long. That it is not made in the U K is perhaps because its economic superiority is much less in low wage European countries than in the U S, and the pressure on European entrepreneurs to use it is therefore less. Machinery manufacturing firms in the U K might therefore believe that the initial U K market for machinery of the U S type would be too small to allow their overheads to be covered. U S machinery manufacturers have an immediate market for superior machinery since they know that the pressure on entrepreneurs to use it once it is available will be considerable because of the high wage. Machinery manufacturers in Europe may be in a less fortunate position, and therefore have less inducement to offer more expensive and efficient machinery of the U S type for sale. Alternatively, as a result of the smaller European market for machinery of the U S type, its cost of production might be more than 30% higher in Europe than in the U S, in which case it would be cheaper to import it from the U S, in spite of the tariff, than to manufacture it in Europe.

It would follow from this argument that capital goods such as A would be more used in the U K if the tariff against machinery was removed. In addition, if 'pay-roll' taxes made labour more expensive, their use in the U K would give machinery manufacturers more incentive to offer machinery such as A for sale, because entrepreneurs would be under more pressure to use it.

The effect of the real wage on the technique of production appears to lie mainly in the way in which it makes a false choice particularly expensive in a country where it is high. Technical progress may be stimulated in such countries since entrepreneurs may be forced to purchase superior machinery soon after it becomes available, and machinery manufacturers may therefore have a ready market for superior products. The superior machinery which is used in consequence is not used throughout the world, partly because of tariffs, partly because of factors such as entrepreneurial inefficiency and smaller markets in countries where the wage is lower, and partly because the cost of not using it is less in countries where the wage is lower.

The rate of profit and the technique of production

The effect of the rate of profit on the technique of production will now be considered. The choice between C (the technique supposedly used in the U K) and B, another technique with a higher capital output ratio will be considered. A was unambiguously superior to C, i.e., it was superior at every wage rate and every profit rate. It will be seen that while labour productivity is higher with B than with C, it is only more profitable to use B in certain circumstances, and these circumstances will now be analysed.

C costs £6,400, and produces net output which sells for £1,600. It is supposed that B (which is also worked by one worker) costs £10,400 and produces net output which sells for £2,000. The higher capital cost of B and its higher net output could be due to a number of causes. The simplest would be that B is a more complicated machine which does work which has to be performed by hand with C, and as a result of this, it would cost more and output per worker with it would be higher. It might also be more durable than C, in which case its capital cost would be higher (to pay for the more durable materials and the greater accuracy required), and its annual depreciation would be less than C's, so that *net* output with it would be higher. It might also require a longer gestation period than C (i.e., a longer time to manufacture it and bring it into use), and then it would cost more than C because the profit element in the capital cost of manufacturing it would be higher,[1] and it would produce more because the final machine was superior.

Labour productivity is 25% higher with B than with C, so an economy with a constant labour force which used C would have 25% growth in addition to growth made possible by technical progress if its workers were re-equipped with B. In the terminology of Chapter 1, the GG line of an economy using B would be 25% higher than the GG line of an economy using C. There would be more than 25% extra growth from the substitution of B for C if the high investment necessary for this raised the rate of technical progress, or allowed economies of scale to be exploited to a greater extent than before. Without these possible extra benefits, £4,000 of extra investment would be needed to equip a worker with B instead of C, and £400 of extra net output per annum would result from this, so the relevant marginal capital output ratio would be 10 : 1 in the absence of extra technical progress and economies of scale. Then 10% of the NNP would need to be added to net investment to raise the growth rate by 1% per annum. Where an economy's labour force was equipped with C, there would then be considerable opportunity to achieve extra growth through greater investment by substituting B for C, an increase in the share of investment of 1% raising the growth rate by at least $\frac{1}{10}$%. This extra investment opportunity would continue until all workers were equipped with B, and at this point output would be at least 25% higher than it would have been if the labour force had been equipped entirely with C. The possibility of faster growth than that permitted by technical progress would then depend on a switch to a technique superior to B.

If it became more profitable to use B than C, entrepreneurs would be likely to order B instead of C whenever they invested, and B would eventually be used exclusively. The circumstances where B would be more profitable than C will now be considered.

[1] See David Ricardo's, *Principles of Political Economy and Taxation*, 3rd edition, 1821, Chapter 1, iv (reprinted as Volume 1 of *Works and Correspondence of David Ricardo*, edited P. Sraffa, Cambridge University Press, 1953).

The argument will relate to just one country, and it will be assumed that both capital goods and their products are manufactured and sold domestically. For simplicity, it will be assumed in the text of this chapter that workers in the capital and consumer goods industries are equipped with capital of equal cost. This assumption ensures that the relative prices of capital and consumer goods will be the same at all rates of profit[1] which much simplifies the argument. The effect on the argument of relaxing this assumption will be outlined in Appendix I to this chapter.

It might be thought that B would be more profitable than C if the rate of interest was low enough. It is supposed to start with that the interest rate has no effect on the cost of B and C, or on the amounts for which their net outputs are sold, and that it has no effect on the wage which is assumed to be £900. In Table 3.5 the relative profitability of B and C is compared when the interest rate is 6% and 4%.

TABLE 3.5

W	K	Q	P	r	Interest rate i	r–i
£900	C £6,400 B £10,400	£1,600 £2,000	£700 £1,100	10·9% 10·6%	6% 6%	4·9% 4·6%
£900	C £6,400 B £10,400	£1,600 £2,000	£700 £1,100	10·9% 10·6%	4% 4%	6·9% 6·6%

Here C is more profitable than B by 0·3%, whether the interest rate is 6% or 4%. Indeed, on the assumption that the interest rate has no effect on wages or prices, the profit rates which can be earned with B and C, and the difference between them, will be the

[1] If there was a particular money wage, profit per worker with particular equipment would be higher when the rate of profit was higher. If capital per worker was higher in the capital goods industries than in the consumer goods industries, a higher rate of profit would raise profit per worker more in the capital than in the consumer goods industries, so it would raise prices more in the capital goods industries. Then the relative prices of capital and consumer goods would be different at different profit rates. If, however, capital per worker was the same in the capital and consumer goods industries, a higher profit rate would raise prices equally in both, and the relative prices of capital and consumer goods would be the same at all profit rates.

same at every interest rate.[1] If the profit rate with C is r_c and with B r_b and the interest rate is i, the profit rate net of interest is (r_c-i) with C and (r_b-i) with B, and (r_c-i) must exceed (r_b-i) by (r_c-r_b), whatever i is. In the example in Table 3.5, r_c exceeds r_b by 0·3%, so C will be more profitable than B by 0·3% at every interest rate.

It would be wrong to conclude from this example that the interest rate can have no effect on the technique of production. It was argued in Chapter 1 that the profit rate would exceed the interest rate by the margin entrepreneurs required to cover risk, if the supply of finance was elastic. Hence, if the interest rate was lower, competition between entrepreneurs would ensure that the profit rate would also be lower. Hence, with a lower interest rate, prices would be lower, relative to wages. In Table 3.6 the relative profitability of B and C is again compared at interest rates of 6% and 4%, but it is assumed in this table that (for simplicity) prices are 10% lower when the interest rate is 4%, while the wage is £900 at both interest rates. Thus the cost of B and C and their net outputs (i.e., the amounts for which their net outputs are sold) are 10% lower when the interest rate is 4% than when it is 6%.

TABLE 3.6

W	K	Q	P	r	i	(r–i)
£900	C £6,400 B £10,400	£1,600 £2,000	£700 £1,100	10·9% 10·6%	6% 6%	4·9% 4·6%
£900	C £5,760 B £9,360	£1,440 £1,800	£540 £900	9·4% 9·6%	4% 4%	5·4% 5·6%

[1] It might be thought that a lower interest rate would increase the 'present value' of expected future profits which might be discounted back to the present at the interest rate, and that this would alter the relative profitability of B and C. If the profit rate exceeded the interest rate because of risk (while the supply of finance was elastic), expected future profits should be discounted back to the present at the profit rate, not the interest rate, because risk should enter into the discounting rate used. If the profit rate exceeded the interest rate because of inelasticity in the supply of finance, expected future profits should again be discounted back to the present at the profit rate, because the profit rate (not the interest rate) is the opportunity cost of finance. Then, in either case, if the profit rate is unaltered as in Table 3.5, the discounted value of expected future profits will also be unaltered.

Here C is more profitable than B where the interest rate is 6%, but B is more profitable than C where the interest rate is 4%. This is because prices are assumed to be lower relative to wages when the interest rate is lower.

Thus, if a lower interest rate had no effect on wages or prices (as in Table 3.5), it would leave the rates of profit earned with B and C and their relative profitability unaltered. If, on the other hand, it affected prices (as in Table 3.6), it would affect their relative profitability.[1]

In Table 3.6, r is lower with both B and C when the interest rate is lower, and it is lower to a greater extent with the technique where the cost of equipping a worker is less (C), so the relative profitability of the technique where the cost of equipping a worker is higher (B) is raised, and entrepreneurs are therefore more likely to invest in it. It is the lower profit rate due to lower prices in relation to wages which actually makes the relative profitability of B greater. The lower profit rate was supposedly due to a lower interest rate in Table 3.6, but the profit rate could equally be lower (with the same effect) if wages were higher in relation to prices, because of, say, greater long run labour scarcity.

TABLE 3.7

W	K	Q	P	r
£900	C £6,400 B £10,400	£1,600 £2,000	£700 £1,100	10·9% 10·6%
£990	C £6,400 B £10,400	£1,600 £2,000	£610 £1,010	9·5% 9·7%

[1] Businessmen are sometimes said to say that the interest rate has little influence on their investment decisions. (See, for instance, *Oxford Studies in the Price Mechanism*, edited by T. Wilson and P. W. S. Andrews, Oxford University Press, 1951, Chapter 1.) As well as being asked whether the interest rate influences their investment decisions, they should also be asked whether the interest rate influences prices. If it does, it will influence investment decisions since the relative profitability of different techniques of production is different when prices are higher or lower in relation to wages. A businessman would need to be very sophisticated to tell an enquirer who simply asked him whether a reduction in interest rates would influence his investment: 'If the interest rate fell, my costs of production would fall, and competition would force me to lower my prices. At these lower prices, it would pay me to use more capital to produce a unit of output, so if my market was unchanged, I would spend more on capital investment.'

In Table 3.7 the relative profitability of B and C is compared where the wage is £900 and £990 (i.e., 10% higher than £900), while prices (including the prices of capital equipment) are the same at both wage rates.

Here C is more profitable than B where the wage is £900, and B is more profitable than C where the wage is £990. Moreover, the effect of a 10% higher wage on the relative profitability of B and C is the same as the effect 10% lower prices had in Table 3.6. The reason for this is quite simple.

Suppose the wage rises by £50 while prices are unchanged. The profit from employing a worker must then fall by £50 with every technique of production. It costs £6,400 to equip a worker with C, and if the profit from employing a worker falls £50 as a result of a £50 rise in the wage, the rate of profit earned with C must fall by $\frac{£50}{£6,400}$ or 0·8%. It costs £10,400 to equip a worker with B, and if the profit from employing a worker falls by £50, the rate of profit earned with B must fall by $\frac{£50}{£10,400}$ or 0·5%. Thus a £50 rise in wages (while prices are unchanged) must reduce the rate of profit with C by 0·8%, and with B by only 0·5%. It costs substantially less to equip a worker with C; so a rise in wages (while prices are unchanged) which will reduce profit per worker equally with B and C must always reduce *the rate of profit* with C substantially more than *the rate of profit* with B.[1] A fall in prices in relation to wages would have exactly the same effect. Then a sufficient rise in wages in relation to prices, or a sufficient fall in prices in relation to wages can always make a more capitally intensive technique (i.e., a technique where the cost of equipping a worker is greater) more profitable than a less capitally intensive technique, provided the more capitally intensive technique is not unambiguously inferior. This is because the rise in wages (or fall in prices) will least reduce the rate of profit with techniques where the cost of equipping a worker is highest.

It should not be concluded from this argument that the relative profitability of B is necessarily increased when money or real wages are higher. In Table 3.8 the relative profitability of B and C is compared where the wage is £900 and £990, but here when the wage is 10% higher, the cost of B and C and the value of their net

[1] See Professor Joan Robinson's, *The Accumulation of Capital*, Macmillan, 1956, Chapter 10 and bookmarker.

outputs are also assumed to be 10% higher. This situation could be one where the higher wage has simply resulted in 10% price inflation (which would increase the cost of B and C and the money value of their net outputs by 10%). It could also be one where there has been 10% 'neutral' technical progress which has increased the quantity of net output produced by B and C by 10% (while prices are unchanged), increased the cost of equipping a worker with B and C by 10%, and the wage by 10%.

TABLE 3.8

W	K	Q	P	r
£900	C £6,400 B £10,400	£1,600 £2,000	£700 £1,100	10·9% 10·6%
£990	C £7,040 B £11,440	£1,760 £2,200	£770 £1,210	10·9% 10·6%

Here the rates of profit earned with B and C and their relative profitability are unchanged when wages are 10% higher, and capital cost and the amount for which the output of a worker is sold are also 10% higher, so higher money wages which are simply passed on in higher prices,[1] or higher wages which are simply a consequence of 'neutral' technical progress do not affect the relative profitability of B and C. The relative profitability of B will only be raised if wages rise more than prices and productivity, i.e., if wage costs per unit of output rise more than prices.

If wage costs per unit of output rise more than prices, the rate of profit will be reduced with all techniques of production, and it will be reduced most with the techniques where the cost of equipping a worker is least. Thus a rise in wage costs per unit of

[1] It also follows from this result that a 'pay-roll' tax of 10% would have no effect on the relative profitability of B and C if it led to a 10% rise in prices, since there would then be a 10% rise in the cost of labour to entrepreneurs, and in K and Q as in Table 3.8. Moreover, if it led to 10% higher prices, a 'pay-roll' tax would not raise the *real* cost of labour, so it would not have a beneficial effect on productivity. It follows that increased 'pay-roll' taxation and reduced profits taxation must be introduced simultaneously. Then lower rates of profits taxation should lead to lower prices relative to labour costs, and so to increased relative profitability of B, and a higher *real* cost of labour. This will be considered in more detail in Chapter 6.

output in relation to prices, or a fall in prices in relation to wage costs per unit of output will increase the relative profitability of B. A change in the interest rate which leaves wages and prices unaltered, a rise in wages which simply results in higher money prices, or a rise in wages with an equal rise in productivity will not.

Thus, it appears that an increase in wage costs per unit of output in relation to prices is needed if the relative profitability of B is to rise so that entrepreneurs will be persuaded to invest in it. This rise in wage costs per unit of output in relation to prices will always reduce the rate of profit with all techniques of production, but it will reduce it most where the cost of equipping a worker is least. Hence, higher wage costs per unit of output in relation to prices always imply that the rate of profit is lower, so it can either be said that the relative profitability of techniques of production with high capital output ratios is raised when wage costs per unit of output are higher (in relation to prices), or that their relative profitability is raised when the rate of profit is lower.

Conclusion

There are two ways in which the growth rate of a developed economy could be raised through increased capital intensity, i.e., through increases in capital per worker. First, any developed economy apart from the U S could achieve substantially faster growth by making more use of U S production methods. Capital goods with the same capital output ratio as European capital equipment, which permit production with, on average, about twice their labour productivity are used in the U S economy, so Western European economies could have up to 100% of exceptional growth if they could simply duplicate U S production methods, and U S machinery. Among the steps which would be helpful here would be the abolition of tariffs against foreign machinery, and perhaps the use of 'pay-roll' taxes, which would make labour more expensive to Western European entrepreneurs if they were not fully passed on, and so increase the pressure to use capital goods permitting production with higher labour productivity.[1]

The other way in which growth rates could be raised through increased capital intensity would be through reductions in the rate

[1] Some Western European economies have taken important steps in this direction since 1945. See P.E.P. *The Promotion of Economic Growth*, March 1961, and Sir Robert Shone's 'Economic development of the United Kingdom Steel Industry', *Journal of the Royal Society of Arts*, July 1961.

of profit (and increases in wage costs per unit of output relative to prices), which would increase the incentive to use techniques with higher capital output ratios. Here the relevant marginal capital output ratio for growth might be as high as 100 : r (where r is the rate of profit),[1] and consequently a great deal of extra investment would probably be needed for quite moderate increases in the rate of growth.

There is a reservation to the argument of this chapter which might be important. It has been argued throughout that capital intensity is determined by entrepreneurs who decide on the most profitable combination of *labour* and *capital*. The effect on capital intensity of factors of production other than labour and capital has been ignored. It is, however, possible to take a completely different view of capital intensity. It could be argued that in some fundamental sense, a certain amount of energy, human or mechanical, is needed to turn raw materials into finished goods. The alternative to using only labour (i.e., human energy) is the use of some other kind of energy in place of labour. Coal, oil, and nuclear power can be used to produce electricity, and machinery is needed to exploit the energy obtainable from this. If energy is obtainable much more cheaply from electricity (or steam) than from workers, it would become profitable to use cheap electricity (or steampower) in place of labour. The invention of machinery which allows production with high labour productivity might then be partly a consequence of cheap fuel in relation to labour. The essential factor leading to the substitution of mechanical power for labour might sometimes then be the relative cost of fuel and labour, not capital and labour, and the use of a large quantity of capital per worker would then be a consequence of cheap fuel in relation to labour.[2]

If there is some substance to this line of thought, there would be added reason for superior U S productivity. Coal deposits are

[1] See n. 1, p. 17.

[2] The argument that fuel costs might sometimes have a significant effect on capital intensity was first suggested to me by Sir Robert Shone. The possibility that the relative costs of fuel and labour might significantly influence capital intensity has been largely neglected in economic theory, perhaps partly because it is defined out of account where land, labour, capital and entrepreneurship are regarded as *the* 'factors of production'. Labour and capital are 'factors of production', so there can obviously be substitution between them, but fuel (which is presumably part of 'land') is not nearly so obviously a 'factor of production', so substitution of fuel for labour is not seen as a clear possibility.

greatly superior and much more accessible in the US than the UK (and this is true of oil *a fortiori*), and labour productivity in the US coal mining industry has consequently always been much higher. Labour productivity in US coal mining is perhaps *three* or *four* times as high as in the UK,[1] so coal might cost one quarter or one-third as much (in relation to labour) in the US, and electricity would also then be much cheaper. This might encourage (and might have encouraged) the development of US machinery which used more fuel and less labour to produce a unit of output. This machinery would be less profitable in the UK, where electricity is dearer and labour cheaper.

With this line of argument, the price of electricity to industry could have a particularly important effect on labour productivity. Increases in the price of electricity to industry might lead to lower capital intensity in some industries, as well as directly leading to higher costs of production in world markets.

This line of argument will not be pursued further in this book, and the more usual view that raising capital intensity is essentially a matter of substituting capital rather than fuel for labour will be taken in the remaining chapters.

APPENDIX I

The rate of profit, and relative prices of capital and consumer goods

In the text of the chapter, it was assumed that the relative prices of capital and consumer goods would be the same at all profit rates, because the cost of equipping a worker was assumed to be the same in the capital and consumer goods industries. For this reason, when, for instance, the effect of a lower profit rate resulting from a lower interest rate was considered in Table 3.6, the prices of both capital and consumer goods were reduced by 10%, so the cost of B and C and the money value of their net outputs were reduced by 10%. However, if the workers in the capital goods industries were equipped with capital which cost twice as much as capital in the consumer goods industries, a lower profit rate would lead to price reductions which were about twice as great in the capital goods industries as those in the consumer goods

[1] Productivity in US coal mining was 3·81 times as high as in the UK in 1938. See Rostas, op. cit., p. 81.

industries. If capital per worker was twice as great in the consumer goods industries, competition would ensure that price reductions following a lower profit rate were approximately twice as great in the consumer goods industries as those in the capital goods industries. Clearly a rise in wage costs per unit of output relatively to prices would have a similar effect on relative prices.

Then, if capital per worker was higher in the capital goods industries, a lower profit rate would have two effects on the relative profitability of B and C. First, the relative profitability of B would be increased through the normal effect of a lower profit rate which was analysed in the text of the chapter. Second, if capital per worker was higher in the capital goods industries, a lower profit rate would mean that capital goods prices were reduced more than consumer goods prices, so capital would be cheaper in terms of consumer goods. If entrepreneurs in the consumer goods industries could buy capital equipment more cheaply (in terms of their own products), they would have an added incentive to increase capital per worker.[1] Hence, entrepreneurs would have a double incentive to use B, a technique of production with a higher capital output ratio than C, when the rate of profit was lower. They would have the normal incentive to use B instead of C because of a lower rate of profit, and they would have an added incentive because capital goods were cheaper in terms of the goods they produced. Hence, where capital per worker is higher in the capital goods industries, entrepreneurs would have greater incentives to use B instead of C than the argument of the text of the chapter suggested.[2]

[1] This effect is analysed in detail in my 'Capital cost and the choice of technique', *Bulletin of the Oxford University Institute of Economics and Statistics*, 1963.

[2] When capital per worker is higher in the capital goods industries, the cost of capital goods is lower relatively to the cost of consumer goods when the rate of profit is lower, so the capital output ratio of particular capital goods is also lower. It is then conceivable that B's capital output ratio might become lower than C's original capital output ratio of 4:1. B's original capital output ratio is 5·2:1, and if consumer goods prices became 20% lower and capital goods prices 40% lower, its capital output ratio would fall to 3·9:1. Hence a *much* lower profit rate could lead to the use of a technique with more physical capital per worker, i.e., to the use of B instead of C; but to a fall in the capital output ratio, since C would be used at a high profit rate, and its capital output ratio would then be 4:1, while B would be used at a much lower profit rate, and its capital output ratio would then be 3·9:1. The lower profit rate would then be associated with production with a *lower* capital output ratio (if B and C were the only techniques). This is an extreme possibility, and it can only occur where capital per worker is much higher in the capital goods industries (when the opposite is much more often the case). It will consequently be neglected in the main text of the book, where it will be presumed that use of techniques with more capital per worker when the rate of profit is lower will always involve production with a higher capital output ratio.

In the converse situation where capital per worker is less in the capital goods industries, a lower profit rate would cheapen consumer goods more than capital goods. Entrepreneurs in the consumer goods industries would then find that the cost of capital goods was reduced less than the prices for which they could sell consumer goods, so the relative cost of their capital would be increased. This would (taken by itself) dissuade them from increasing capital per worker. On the other hand, the lower profit rate would increase the relative profitability of B in the way outlined in the text of the chapter. Here the incentive to use B instead of C when the rate of profit is lower would be weakened. In an extreme case, the lower prices of consumer goods relative to capital goods could altogether wipe out the incentive to use B instead of C.

In the UK and the US, capital per worker is generally higher in the consumer goods industries, because capital per worker is generally low in the building and machinery producing industries, and consequently capital goods would generally become more expensive relative to consumer goods at a lower profit rate. This would be likely to counteract part of the incentive to adopt more capitally intensive techniques which would normally follow from a lower profit rate.

There is one further possible complication to the argument. It has been taken for granted up to now that when the rate of profit is lower, all capital goods are reduced in cost equally, and this would be the case if all the workers who manufactured capital goods were equipped with the same amount of capital. The workers who manufacture the more capitally intensive B might, however, be equipped with more capital than the workers who manufacture C, and then, if the rate of profit was lower, the price of B would be reduced relatively to the price of C, and the incentive to adopt B would be increased; while it would be reduced if more capital per worker was needed to manufacture C. In an extreme case, where D was a technique with a lower capital output ratio than C, and much more capital per worker was needed to manufacture it than either B or C, a lower profit rate might reduce its cost so much in relation to the cost of B and C that entrepreneurs would have an incentive to switch from C to D when the profit rate was lower instead of from C to the more capitally intensive B.[1]

[1] See Professor Joan Robinson, op. cit., pp. 109–10. It might be thought that this is an improbable 'perverse' case, because, in general, the capital needed for techniques with higher capital output ratios would itself be manufactured with more capital per worker (and this is the situation in Ricardo's analysis, op. cit., Chapter 1, v), but it might often be the case that capital with a low capital output ratio could be mass produced (for instance, standard lathes), while capital with higher capital output ratios (for instance, machinery for automation) might be demanded in insufficient quantity to justify mass production, so it might be manufactured largely by skilled labour using little capital per worker.

A lower profit rate would increase the incentive to use B, a technique with a higher capital output ratio, in place of C, apart from two 'perverse' cases which have been outlined above. It would not necessarily do so if consumer goods were manufactured with much more capital per worker than capital goods,[1] and it would not necessarily do so where the capital needed for techniques with lower capital output ratios than C (such as D) was manufactured with much more capital, so that a lower rate of profit cheapened D so much relatively to C that entrepreneurs had an incentive to switch from C to D instead of from C to B. Apart from these 'perverse' cases (and they will be neglected in the main text of the book), a lower profit rate (with consequently higher wage costs per unit of output relative to prices) would always increase the incentive to use techniques of production with a higher capital output ratio, but such incentives are always weakened where capital per worker is higher in the consumer goods industries than in the capital goods industries which manufacture their equipment, and strengthened where it is lower.

APPENDIX II

The 'Cobb–Douglas' production function

Wicksell occasionally used a particular mathematical function to relate output to capital intensity which has been taken up by a number of authors since C. W. Cobb and Professor Paul H. Douglas discovered it independently of Wicksell in 1928.[2]

In this function, it is assumed that output varies with C, the amount of capital used, raised to an exponential power of 'a' where 'a' is less

[1] This 'perverse' case does not appear in *The Accumulation of Capital.* It could occur in the following way in Professor Joan Robinson's diagrams (figures 1 and 2 on pp. 412–13). The production function shifts to the left when the rate of profit is lower (i.e., from $\alpha_3\beta_3\gamma_3\delta_3$ to $\alpha_2\beta_2\gamma_2\delta_2$ in figure 2), which, taken by itself, would cause a line from the original N to be tangential at a lower technique; but N also shifts to the left when the rate of profit is lower, which, taken by itself, causes a line from it to be tangential at a higher technique. She takes it for granted that the latter effect would outweigh the former, but there is no reason why it should always do so.

[2] C. W. Cobb and Paul H. Douglas, 'A theory of production', *American Economic Review Supplement,* Vol XVIII, March 1928. The function is to be found in Wicksell's *Lectures on Political Economy,* Routledge and Kegan Paul, 1934 (the lectures were published in Sweden in 1901), Vol 1, p. 128, and on p. 286 of Vol 1 where it is used in his 'A Mathematical Analysis of Dr Akerman's problem'.

than 1, and with the amount of labour used, L, raised to an exponential power of 'b' where b is less than 1. Output Q then equals A (which is a constant) times C^a times L^b, i.e., $Q=A.C^a.L^b$. Because a and b are less than 1, the function takes account of diminishing returns to labour and capital when one is increased and the other is constant. For instance, if $a=\frac{1}{2}$, and capital is doubled while labour is constant, output increases from $A.C^{\frac{1}{2}}.L^b$ to $A.(2C)^{\frac{1}{2}}.L^b$, or to $2^{\frac{1}{2}}$ times $A.C^{\frac{1}{2}}.L^b$. Thus when capital alone is doubled, output increases $2^{\frac{1}{2}}$ or 1.414 times. Where 'a' has any value less than 1, doubling capital increases output 2^a times which must result in less than doubling of output since 2^a must be less than 2 where a is less than 1. Similarly, doubling the labour force less than doubles output when b is less than 1. The function has the further property that when (a+b) equals 1, there are constant returns to labour and capital when both are increased in the same proportion. For example, doubling labour and capital increases output from $A.C^a.L^b$ to $A.(2C)^a.(2L)^b$ which equals $2^a.2^b$ times $A.C^a.L^b$. Output is thus increased $2^a.2^b$ times or $2^{(a+b)}$ times, which equals 2 when $(a+b)=1$. If (a+b) is greater than 1, doubling labour and capital would more than double output, since $2^{(a+b)}$ would exceed 2, and a situation where (a+b) exceeded 1 would correspond to 'increasing returns' to labour and capital, while an (a+b) of less than 1 would correspond to 'diminishing returns' to labour and capital. The authors who have used the production function have generally assumed constant returns to labour and capital (when they are increased together), and they have consequently assumed that (a+b) equalled 1. They could then write (1−a) for b, and the production function can then be written down as $Q=A.C^a.L^{(1-a)}$.

In this form the function has another property (which will not be appreciated by readers who are unfamiliar with 'differentiation' who are therefore advised to miss this paragraph). When output, Q, is partially differentiated with respect to capital, $\frac{dQ}{dC}$ or the marginal product of capital becomes $A.a.C^{(a-1)}.L^{(1-a)}$ which equals $\frac{Q.a}{C}$; and when it is partially differentiated with respect to labour, $\frac{dQ}{dL}$ or the marginal product of labour becomes $A.(1-a).C^a.L^{-a}$ which equals $\frac{Q(1-a)}{L}$. If the rate of profit equals the marginal product of capital, it equals $\frac{Q.a}{C}$, and total profits must equal C times the rate of profit, or Q.a. If the wage equals the marginal product of labour, it equals $\frac{Q(1-a)}{L}$, and total wages must equal L times the wage, or Q(1−a). Then total wages plus total profits equal Q(1−a) plus Q.a, or Q, if the rate of profit equals the marginal product of capital and the wage equals the marginal product of labour. Hence the function is consistent with the marginal productivity theory of distribution in so far as, when each factor is paid its marginal product, total payments to factors equal total output when there are constant returns to scale.

Hence the function appears to have much to recommend it at first sight. It takes account of the possibility of diminishing returns to factors of production when they are increased individually and of constant returns when they are increased together, and in addition, it is consistent with the marginal productivity theory of distribution when its form is $Q=A.C^{a}.L^{(1-a)}$.

While Wicksell merely used the function as a theoretical device which he applied to situations where there was no technical progress, and only one kind of capital such as axes, Cobb and Douglas believed it could be applied to actual economies. They showed that when it was applied to US manufacturing output between 1899 and 1922, the facts fitted the theory remarkably closely when 'a' had a value of 0.25. This was a remarkable statistical achievement, because there is no allowance for technical progress in this form of the function, so if this statistical verification was correct, it would have meant that there was no technical progress at all in the US economy between 1899 and 1922. The function was applied to other economies, and to the US economy in other periods, and values of 'a' of between 0.1 and 0.5 were found.[1] Professor Douglas believed in 1948[1] that these applications went a long way towards demonstrating the correspondence of the function to the actual world. Every successful demonstration implied that there was no technical progress in the actual world.

In recent years, the further term e^{tn} has been added to the function to take account of technical progress, where 100.t% is approximately equal to the rate of technical progress, and n is the year in question. Then output in year n, Q_n, equals $A.e^{tn}.C^{a}.L^{(1-a)}$. e^{tn} grows by approximately 100.t% per annum, so the effect of the insertion of this term is that output grows by 100.t% per annum as a result of technical progress, whatever the rate of investment may be. If there is any net investment, C is increased, so output is increased by net investment in addition. The insertion of this term does not affect the relation between the function and the laws of returns, and the marginal productivity theory of distribution. In this form it is less indefensible than in the form where technical progress is left out of account altogether, but it still has a number of notable defects.

There is one defect which is not fundamental, since modification of the function could correct it. The way in which technical progress is treated is obviously a serious defect because it is assumed that no

[1] Professor Douglas, 'Are there laws of production?', *American Economic Review*, March 1948. There is a summary there of applications of the function to various economies over various periods.

investment is needed to take advantage of technical progress, i.e., that all technical progress is 'disembodied'. In the actual world there is certainly some 'disembodied' technical progress, but much technical progress will require investment because newly designed capital goods will be needed to take advantage of new knowledge, and the function makes no allowance for such 'embodied' technical progress. An important consequence follows from the assumption that all technical progress is 'disembodied'. Since it is assumed that full advantage can be taken of technical progress without investment, net investment is always subject to diminishing returns. The result is that the importance of investment in exploiting the opportunities for growth created by technical progress is greatly understated. This defect could be overcome if the function was given a different mathematical form, but there are other fundamental defects.[1]

It appears at first sight that the relationship between a lower rate of profit, a consequently higher capital output ratio, and consequently higher output could be read off very simply from the function if 'a' was known. If the rate of profit is lower, the marginal product of capital must be lower to the same extent, and this equals $a.\frac{Q}{C}$. The change in $\frac{Q}{C}$ must then be proportional to the change in the rate of profit, and the effect of changes in $\frac{Q}{C}$ on Q can be read off quite simply from the function. The difficulty that capital cost changes when the rate of profit changes (which was considered in Appendix I) appears to be avoided, but it is not. C and Q must clearly be measured in the same units. Measuring in units of Q, C must usually change in value when the rate of profit changes, because the prices of capital goods change relative to the prices of consumer goods when the rate of profit changes if there is a difference between capital per worker in the capital and consumer goods industries. If C changes in relation to Q when the rate of profit changes, the rate of profit (and the marginal product of capital) cannot possibly equal $\frac{dQ}{dC}$, because C alters in valuation relatively to Q whenever the marginal product of capital changes. Then the term $\frac{dQ}{dC}$ only has a clear meaning where capital per worker is the same in the capital and consumer goods industries.

A further fundamental defect is that while C consists partly of new capital goods, it consists mostly of old capital goods, and some way must be found of valuing the old capital in relation to the new capital. The output produced by old capital (measured in current prices) changes whenever there is technical progress in the industry concerned,

[1] Readers unfamiliar with differentiation should miss the next paragraph.

whenever wages and prices change, when capital deteriorates and when the rate of profit changes. The effects of the deterioration of capital and of technical obsolescence may be foreseen by entrepreneurs to some extent when they calculate their depreciation, but the other effects cannot be forecast. Moreover in most actual economies the official depreciation figures which are used by the statisticians who calculate C depend on arbitrary tax allowances (such as that capital can be written off in ten years), and not on the life and pattern of output entrepreneurs expect their capital to have. Hence there are bound to be serious errors in the valuation of old capital, and these errors are not of the kind which cancel out (any more than the errors would cancel out if a hundred Englishmen were asked to guess the distance from Omsk to Tomsk and their answers were averaged). There would be a definite bias in the calculations if technical progress was other than at the expected rate, if there was a change in the rate of profit, or if the figures were in any way affected by arbitrary fiscal regulations. These defects in any measurement of C are inescapable.

Thus, apart from the situation where capital per worker is the same in the capital and consumer goods industries, $\frac{dQ}{dC}$ is a concept without a clear meaning (since the measurement of C in units of Q would not be independent of $\frac{dQ}{dC}$), and C is immensely difficult to measure. These difficulties do not apply to the 'Cobb–Douglas' production function alone. They apply wherever all the capital in an economy is aggregated into an algebraic term such as 'C', and they apply wherever the term 'marginal productivity of capital' is used.

4

ECONOMIC GROWTH AT FULL EMPLOYMENT

Introduction

It has been taken for granted so far in the argument that the level of demand will always permit full employment. In this chapter, the conditions necessary for this will be examined. In Chapter 1 it was argued that when the rate of profit is given, there is a limit to the amount it is profitable to invest in an economy. Suppose that limit is 12% of the full employment NNP. Then it would be unprofitable to invest 13% of the NNP at full employment, or 14% or 15%, but it is not at all inconceivable that people and firms together might wish to save 13%, 15%, or even 25% of the NNP. If they wished to save more than 12% of the NNP, while only 12% of the NNP could be invested profitably, there would be insufficient demand to permit the maintenance of full employment. There would then be unemployment, the NNP would consequently be lower than at full employment, and the amount people would wish to save would also be lower as a result of the lower incomes consequent on a lower NNP. The amount of unemployment would be such that the amount people and firms wished to save (out of their lower incomes) would equal the amount which was invested.[1]

Thus the primary condition which needs to be satisfied before full employment can be maintained is that at full employment, the percentage of the NNP which people and firms wish to save must not exceed the percentage it is profitable to invest.

However, if entrepreneurs failed to take full advantage of profitable investment opportunities, the above condition would not be sufficient, because it might then be profitable to invest 12%

[1] This is an elementary proposition in 'Keynesian' employment theory which will be taken for granted here. It is explained in detail in Professor Joan Robinson's *Introduction to the Theory of Employment*, Macmillan, 1937.

of the NNP, and planned saving at full employment might actually be 12% of the NNP, while actual investment plans might only amount to 10% of the NNP. In this event, full employment could not be maintained, and there would be sufficient unemployment to bring plans to save into line with plans to invest.

Thus, it is quite certain that full employment could not be maintained if it was only profitable to invest 12% of the NNP, and plans to save exceeded 12% of the NNP, but it is not certain that full employment would be maintained if saving plans were less than 12%, because it is not certain that entrepreneurs would actually take advantage of profitable investment opportunities. For the maintenance of full employment, it is necessary both that planned saving at full employment should not exceed profitable investment opportunity, and that entrepreneurs should take advantage of such profitable investment opportunities as there are.

These conditions will be analysed in much more detail in this chapter and in Chapter 5, and the various mechanisms which might bring saving and investment plans together at full employment will be examined.

The 'warranted' rate of growth

It was pointed out in Chapter 1 that where C is defined as the $\frac{\text{increase in capital}}{\text{increase in output}}$ which actually occurs in a given period of time, and S as the $\frac{\text{increase in capital}}{\text{output}}$ in the same period, $\frac{S}{C}$ is the $\frac{\text{increase in output}}{\text{output}}$ in that period, or G, the actual rate of growth. Thus G must equal $\frac{S}{C}$ where S is the *actual* percentage of income saved, and C is the *actual* ratio of net investment to the increase in net output, or the actual capital coefficient. If the period of time is a year, G is the rate of growth of output per annum.

C units are actually added to capital when one unit is added to output, but it might be supposed that entrepreneurs would find it most profitable to use a given amount of capital, C_r units, to produce a unit of output, and C the actual addition to capital when output rose by a unit might well differ from C_r. C_r would depend partly on the ruling rate of profit, partly on technological factors (i.e., the techniques of production actually available), and partly on convenience, since entrepreneurs would have formed views in the past of the amount of capital (including inventories) which they found it most convenient to have to produce one unit of output. C_r would include both the fixed capital and the stocks of finished goods and raw materials which entrepreneurs wished to have to produce a unit of output. If entrepreneurs had the amount of capital they wished to have to produce current output initially, C_r would be the amount they wished to add to their capital when output rose by a unit, and C would be the amount actually added. Then, if C was less than C_r, entrepreneurs would have less capital than they ideally wished to have, and they might well respond by investing an exceptional amount in an endeavour to make good the shortage, while if C was greater than C_r, they would have more capital than they wished to have, and would probably respond by cutting investment to try to get rid of their excess capital. Then entrepreneurs might well raise investment when C was less than C_r, and reduce it when C exceeded C_r.

For example, suppose entrepreneurs wished to use 4 units of capital to produce a unit of output so that C_r was 4, and output increased by £10,000,000. Then, if they had the amount of capital they wished to have before this, they would be satisfied if the increase in output was accompanied by an increase in capital of £40,000,000. However, if C was 3, the actual increase in capital would be £30,000,000 and this would mean that they had £10,000,000 less capital than they wished to have, and their response would almost certainly be an exceptionally high rate of investment in the next period to make good the deficiency. If C was actually 5 so that the actual increase in capital was £50,000,000, they would have £10,000,000 more capital than they wished to have, and would consequently cut investment.

Since $G \equiv \frac{S}{C}$, it is a truism that C must equal $\frac{S}{G}$. If S does not change much when G changes,[1] C must change mainly because of

[1] Where G (the actual rate of growth) rises, S will rise too, and vice versa. When G rises, consumption which is almost certainly partly determined by past levels of income (see, for instance, Professor J. Duesenberry's *Income, Saving and the Theory of Consumer Behaviour*, Harvard, 1952) will rise proportionally less than current incomes; so S, the share of saving, will rise, and in addition, when G rises, the share of profits in income is likely to rise, and this too will cause S to rise because a high proportion of profits is likely to be saved. Similarly, when G falls, S is likely to fall because the rate of growth of consumption would fall less than the rate of growth of incomes, and because the share of profits would fall. It is nevertheless almost certain that the proportionate change in S would be less than the proportionate change in G. To

changes in G. For instance, if S was 20% and G was 4%, C which equals $\frac{S}{G}$ would be 5, while C would become 2 if G became 10% while S remained 20%. Thus when 20% of income is saved, C is 5 when the rate of growth of income is 4%, and 2 when it is 10%. Now suppose C_r is 4. Then, if the actual rate of growth was 10% so that C was 2, C_r which is 4 would be higher than C, so entrepreneurs would eventually raise investment and the rate of growth. On the other hand, if the actual rate of growth was 4% and C was therefore 5 and higher than C_r, entrepreneurs would eventually reduce investment and the rate of growth. If the actual rate of growth was 5%, C would be 4 as well as C_r, and then entrepreneurs would find that the amount actually being added to capital was exactly what they wished it to be.

If the actual rate of growth was at all higher than 5%, C would be less than 4 and therefore less than C_r, so, because it eventually caused a shortage of capital, a growth rate exceeding 5% would almost certainly lead to further increases in the rate of growth. Conversely, a rate of growth of less than 5% would cause C to become higher than C_r and lead to surplus capacity, and so to cuts in investment and the rate of growth. There is only one rate of growth where a continuous rise or fall in the rate of growth could be avoided, and that is where C equals C_r. Since C necessarily equals $\frac{S}{G}$, the rate of growth which causes C to equal C_r must be where $\frac{S}{G}$ equals C_r, or where G equals $\frac{S}{C_r}$. It is only when the actual rate of growth is $\frac{S}{C_r}$ that the actual capital coefficient can equal C_r. If S was 10% and C_r 4, a rate of growth of $\frac{10}{4}$% or $2\frac{1}{2}$% would cause the actual C to equal 4, and if S was 15% and C_r 3, an actual growth rate of $\frac{15}{3}$% or 5% would cause the actual C to equal 3.

---

quote Sir Roy Harrod, 'Without any great revolution G might easily change from 2% to 6%. This clearly could not cause saving to be trebled' (*Towards a Dynamic Economics*, p. 79). In the text, for simplicity, S is held constant when G changes, but all the conclusions of the argument would follow equally if S changed when G changed, provided the proportional change in S was always less than the proportional change in G.

Sir Roy Harrod has called this rate of growth of $\frac{S}{C_r}\%$ the 'warranted' rate of growth, and it is convenient to follow his notation and use the term G_w to describe the 'warranted' rate of growth, in contrast to the term G which refers to the *actual* rate of growth. Then $G_w=\frac{S}{C_r}$ describes the only rate of growth which will allow entrepreneurs to have the amount of capital in relation to output which they actually wish to have. If $G_w=\frac{S}{C_r}$, $G_w.C_r$ must equal S, and since $G\equiv\frac{S}{C}$, GC must also equal S. Then G_wC_r and GC both equal S, so G_wC_r equals GC. Then it can easily be seen that when G is greater than G_w, C must be less than C_r, and vice versa. Thus a G greater than G_w automatically makes C less than C_r, and so leads to a shortage of capital.

Sir Roy Harrod has defined the 'warranted' rate of growth in various ways. In 1939, he defined it as '. . . that rate of growth which, if it occurs, will leave all parties satisfied that they have produced neither more nor less than the right amount'.[1] Clearly they cannot be satisfied of this unless the actual rate of growth is $\frac{S}{C_r}$, because it is only then that they can have the amount of capital in relation to output which they want. In 1948 he defined the 'warranted' rate of growth as '. . . that over-all rate of advance which, if executed, will leave entrepreneurs in a state of mind in which they are prepared to carry on a similar advance'.[2] Here again it is clear that an actual rate of growth which exceeded $\frac{S}{C_r}$ would cause entrepreneurs to become increasingly short of capital, so they would certainly not be left in a state of mind 'in which they would be prepared to carry out a similar advance'. Because of the increasing capital shortage, they would almost certainly wish to carry out a greater rate of advance than before. Similarly, since an actual rate of growth of less than $\frac{S}{C_r}$ would lead to excess capital, it would almost certainly cause entrepreneurs to plan for a slower rate of growth. It is only when the actual rate of

[1] 'An essay in Dynamic Theory,' *Economic Journal*, 1939, p. 16.
[2] *Towards a Dynamic Economics*, p. 82.

growth is $\frac{S}{C_r}$ that Sir Roy's definition of 1948 can possibly be satisfied. Of course, if the actual growth rate was $\frac{S}{C_r}$, it would not necessarily follow that entrepreneurs would continuously plan for the same rate of advance as in the previous period. That their past plans worked out as they expected would not be a sufficient condition to cause them to repeat those plans, but there would not be the slightest chance that they would choose to repeat their plans if they did not work out as expected. Thus the only *possibility* that they would continuously repeat their plans would occur when the rate of growth was $\frac{S}{C_r}$. In 1952 Sir Roy suggested an alternative postulate to describe entrepreneurial behaviour:

Let the representative entrepreneur on each occasion of giving an order repeat the amount contained in his order for the last equivalent period, adding thereto an order for an amount by which he judges his existing stock to be be deficient, if he judges it to be deficient, or subtracting therefrom the amount by which he judges his stock to be redundant, if he does so judge it. Let him judge his stock to be neither redundant nor deficient when it consists of a certain fraction, C, of his intended order.[1]

Where the actual rate of growth is higher than $\frac{S}{C_r}$, C becomes less than C_r, and it would almost certainly follow that the 'representative entrepreneur' would judge his stock to be deficient, and would then, according to this new postulate, increase his orders, and this would raise the actual rate of growth still further above $\frac{S}{C_r}$. Similarly, where the actual rate of growth is less than $\frac{S}{C_r}$, C is higher than C_r and it would almost certainly follow that the 'representative entrepreneur' would judge that part of his stock was redundant, and reduce his orders which would reduce the actual rate of growth still further. The stock of the 'representative entrepreneur' would only be neither deficient nor redundant if the actual rate of growth was $\frac{S}{C_r}$, so that C equalled C_r.

[1] *Economic Essays*, Macmillan, 1952, No 14, p. 284.

Consequently it is perhaps simplest to regard the 'warranted' rate of growth as $\frac{S}{C_r}\%$, where S is the percentage of the NNP which is saved, and C_r is the capital coefficient which entrepreneurs wish to maintain. A rate of growth faster than this must cause C to become less than C_r which must have the effect of eventually causing entrepreneurs to believe that they have produced *less than the right amount*; it is likely to leave entrepreneurs in a state of mind where *they would be prepared to carry out a greater advance than in the previous period*, and it must *cause their stock to be deficient*, while a rate of growth slower than $\frac{S}{C_r}\%$ would have the opposite effects.

The 'warranted' rate of growth and the 'natural' rate

It was argued in Chapter 1 that an actual rate of growth faster than G_n, the 'natural' rate, could only be sustained while moves to higher GG lines were actually taking place.[1] Otherwise a rate of growth faster than G_n would be unprofitable. It was argued above that a rate of growth slower than G_w could not be sustained for long because it would cause C to become higher than C_r, which would cause a continuous fall in the rate of growth. Clearly an economy where the 'warranted' rate of growth was higher than the 'natural' rate would be in a position of great difficulty.

Suppose that G_n is 3%, that C_r is 3 and that S is 15%. Then G_w would be $\frac{15}{3}\%$ or 5%. There are two ways of looking at the difficulties in this situation. First, in simple 'Keynesian' terms, with G_n 3% and C_r 3, it would be impossible to find profitable long-run investment opportunities for more than 9% of the NNP, while, at full employment, 15% of the NNP would be saved. There would then be insufficient investment opportunity to allow full employment to be maintained for long.

The other way of looking at the problem, in terms of Sir Roy Harrod's 'warranted' and 'natural' rates of growth, is very similar. In this argument, when S is 15% and C_r is 3, only an actual growth rate of 5% would keep C equal to 3, so only an actual growth rate of 5% would leave entrepreneurs content, and any rate of growth

[1] A fall in the rate of profit would only permit movement to a higher GG line; so it would only permit growth faster than the 'natural' rate while the move to a higher GG line actually took place.

of less than 5% would cause C to become higher than 3, causing an eventual contraction of investment. With a G_n of only 3%, a 5% growth rate could not be maintained indefinitely when the economy was at full employment, so C would inevitably become higher than 3, and investment and employment would then fall. Thus a G_w which exceeded G_n would necessarily lead to unemployment 'most of the time'.

Where G_n is higher than G_w, there is also difficulty. Suppose there is full employment initially, that G_n is 3% and C_r 3 as before, but that S is 6%. Then it would be potentially profitable to invest 9% of the NNP, but saving would only amount to 6% of the NNP. As was pointed out in Chapter 1, there would then be demand-induced inflationary pressure if entrepreneurs actually tried to invest 9% of the NNP.

Where actual investment is defined as 'that part of output which is not consumed', and actual saving as 'that part of income which is not spent on consumption', *actual* saving must always equal *actual* investment,[1] but *plans* to save may well differ from *plans* to invest. Where *plans* to invest exceed *plans* to save at full employment, as they are likely to when G_n exceeds G_w, there will be demand-induced inflationary pressure. Then, so that *actual* investment can equal *actual* saving, some of the investment plans must be frustrated, or there must be some unplanned saving in addition to planned saving. There are several ways in which actual saving becomes equal to actual investment in an inflationary situation where planned investment exceeds planned saving.

First, there may be delivery delays in the industries making capital goods, or difficulty in obtaining finance, and investment plans would then take longer to carry out than entrepreneurs anticipated; so the investment they *actually* managed to carry out in a year would be less than the amount they had *planned* to carry out. Second, there might be rises in the prices of consumer goods, and some consumers would then be unable to buy all the consumer goods they had planned to buy; so actual consumption would be less than planned consumption, and actual saving more than planned saving.[2] Third, some of the goods people wanted to

[1] Saving (S) is total incomes (Y) less consumption (C). Investment (I) is total output (Q) less consumption (C). Then $S \equiv Y - C$, and $I \equiv Q - C$, so $S \equiv I$ if $Y \equiv Q$, i.e., if total incomes equal total output. This must be true over any period of time. See J. M. Keynes, *The General Theory of Employment Interest and Money*, Macmillan, 1936, p. 63.

[2] Such extra saving caused by rising prices is usually referred to as 'forced saving'.

buy might be unavailable in the shops because of delays in the production and delivery of consumer goods, and this would cause actual consumption to be less than planned consumption, and actual saving to exceed planned saving. Fourth, some of the goods people could not obtain quickly might well be imported (when they were normally produced at home) and goods which could be exported would be diverted to the home market with the result that the current account of the balance of payments would deteriorate, and this would have the same effect as a fall in investment or a rise in saving. Finally, stocks might be run down, and actual investment in stocks would then be less than planned investment. These phenomena need not all occur together, since the entire burden of adjusting investment plans to saving plans could fall, for instance, on the balance of payments, or on delivery delays, but most of them usually occur together.

Then, if G_n exceeded G_w, a likely consequence would be demand-induced inflationary pressure with the above consequences. In simple 'Keynesian' terms, this would be because planned investment exceeded planned saving at full employment with a consequent 'inflationary gap'. In terms of Sir Roy Harrod's equations, where G_n exceeds G_w, G is likely to exceed G_w 'much of the time', and then C would generally be less than C_r which would continuously stimulate expansion. Entrepreneurs' actual expansion would create shortages of fixed capital and of stocks, which would stimulate them to try and expand still faster in circumstances where there was insufficient saving for this. Clearly increases in planned saving would remove the 'inflationary gap' in 'Keynesian' terminology, and bring G_n and G_w together in Sir Roy Harrod's.

If G_n exceeded G_w, and actual investment was less than the amount needed to achieve G_n because of delivery delays, etc, which made actual investment less than planned investment, the life of capital would lengthen. A share of investment of $G_n.C_r$ is needed to maintain a constant life of capital, a capital output ratio of new capital of C_r, and a growth rate of G_n. If the share of saving was less than $G_n.C_r$,[1] the life of capital would necessarily lengthen. The share of saving in the NNP, and therefore the labour and capital available to manufacture capital goods would then be insufficient to permit the production of enough new capital

[1] S must be less than $G_n.C_r$ if G_w is less than G_n. $S = G_w.C_r$, and if G_w is less than G_n, $G_w.C_r$ must be less than $G_n.C_r$; so S must be less than $G_n.C_r$.

goods to keep the life of capital constant with a capital output ratio of C_r. If the life of capital lengthened, the economy would move to a lower GG line; so the actual growth rate would be less than the 'natural' rate because an increasing proportion of the capital stock would become obsolescent.[1] There would, however, be full employment, because there would be more than sufficient demand to allow enough capital, old and new, to be used to equip the entire available labour force. In consequence, where G_n exceeds G_w, there is likely to be continuous full employment with demand inflation, a lengthening of the life of capital because there is insufficient saving to allow a growth rate of G_n to be maintained, and therefore an actual growth rate which would be less than G_n but higher than G_w.

This argument presupposes that there would be sufficient old capital to provide equipment of a kind for the whole labour force. If the labour force is constant, and there is full employment when G_n first exceeds G_w, this must be so, because there is enough capital to equip the whole labour force to start with, and this capital equipment will continue to be used somewhere in the economy if there is sufficient demand, which there certainly will be in this situation. Any gross investment would provide capital equipment for extra workers. If, however, the labour force was growing very quickly, (i.e., if p was very high), and there was no obsolete equipment which could be brought into production, there might be insufficient capital equipment for the whole labour force. If all the existing capital equipment at the beginning of a year was worked throughout the year by the same amount of labour, and there was an increase in the labour force of 3%, there would have to be sufficient new gross investment to provide capital equipment for 3% of the labour force. If, because of lack of saving, and therefore a low G_w, only enough new equipment could be produced to equip 2% more workers, employment could only rise by 2%, and if the labour force rose 3% there would necessarily be 1% unemployment. Unemployment of this kind, due to lack of capital equipment, is usually referred to as 'structural' unemployment. This situation where saving is insufficient to provide enough capital equipment for a rapidly growing labour force may be present in a number of underdeveloped economies.[2]

[1] See p. 27.

[2] See Professor Joan Robinson's, 'Mr Harrod's dynamics', *Economic Journal*, 1949, p. 81.

To sum up the argument so far, there is certain to be insufficient investment opportunity and consequently persistent unemployment if G_w exceeds G_n, and if G_n exceeds G_w, there is bound to be either demand-induced inflation or 'structural' unemployment. To make the position even more difficult, if G, the actual growth rate slightly exceeded G_w, it would tend to increase continuously, while if it was less, it would tend to fall continuously. The result is that unless G, G_n and G_w were exactly equal, which would only happen by chance, there would be a continuous tendency for the rate of growth to fluctuate, and the fluctuations would be around either substantial unemployment, or inflation. The situation in actual economies is not as unfortunate as this because of the possibility of government intervention.

Government influence on S through the budget

Up to this point in the argument, it has been assumed that S is given by the proportion of the NNP which people and firms wish to save. $\frac{S}{C_r}$ is G_w, the only growth rate at which full employment saving can be invested in the long run, and this may differ from G_n with the consequences outlined above. The government can, however, alter S through the budget. If it leaves its expenditure unchanged, and reduces taxes, people and firms will have more money to spend, and they will spend part of it on consumer goods. The proportion of the NNP consumed would then rise, and S, the proportion of the NNP saved would fall. Thus the government can always reduce S by reducing taxes while government expenditure is unchanged. Similarly, if taxes are raised while government expenditure is unchanged, people and firms will have less money to spend, so they are virtually certain to cut their expenditure on consumption to some extent. Then the proportion of the NNP consumed would fall, and S would rise.

There will always be a level of taxation (for each level of government expenditure) where G_w would equal G_n. Suppose G_n was 3% and C_r 3 so that investment opportunity was 9% of the NNP. Suppose that S would be 15% in the absence of government intervention, so that G_w would then be 5%, and exceed G_n. If the government reduced taxes sufficiently to increase consumption by 6% of the NNP, saving would fall from 15% of the NNP to 9%, and G_w would become 3% and equal G_n. Similarly, if S was originally 6% so that G_w was 2%, increased taxation could lead to a reduction in consumption by 3% of the NNP, and so raise S from 6% to 9%, and G_w from 2% to 3%.

Increasing taxation to increase S *might* involve a budget surplus, which would need to be maintained for as long as G_n exceeded G_w. Similarly, reducing taxation to reduce S might require a budget deficit for as long as G_w exceeded G_n. In an economy where balanced budgets were insisted on, this particular method of equating G_n and G_w could not be used, but otherwise budget surpluses or deficits of the requisite size would be the simplest way of equating them.

It will be assumed below that the government's effect on S is neutral, i.e., that this method of equating G_n and G_w is not used. S will then depend, as before, on the proportion of the NNP which people and firms wish to save. The purpose of the analysis will then be to see whether there are other ways in which G_n and G_w may be equated. It is probable that the use of the budget to fix S so that G_w and G_n are equal is the simplest and most obvious way of solving the problems of long-run unemployment or inflation.

Social and 'long range' investment

So far in the argument, it has been taken for granted that all investment is made for profit, and that all capital requires labour to work it. But it is only when investment is made for profit that diminishing returns to capital necessarily set a limit to investment, and it is only when capital requires labour to work it that labour scarcity leads to diminishing returns.

In most economies, about half of all investment is in houses, buildings other than factories, and public works such as roads. Private houses require no employed workers to work them, so the limit to the number of houses in an economy is not set by the size of the labour force. There are, of course, limits set by population, and the amount people wish to spend on housing, but these limits are often imprecise, particularly in a society where many houses are publicly owned and rented, and where part of their cost is paid by the government. If a society decided, through its government, that houses should be larger than before, or that older houses should be replaced, a very substantial amount of investment could be carried out to implement those decisions. With buildings such as schools and hospitals, the number needed cannot be precisely determined, so again there is much flexibility in the number which can be built. With roads, there is no precise mileage which is needed, and few workers are needed to work them, so there is much flexibility in the amount that can be spent on roads in a year.

Suppose that G_w was higher than G_n so that, at full employment, more would be saved than could be profitably invested. In such a situation, investment could be raised if house building, road construction and other public investment was increased. Then investment could equal saving at full employment, and full employment could be maintained. Conversely, if G_n exceeded G_w, cuts in social investment would increase the saving available for investment in industrial plant and machinery.

In the long run, there would obviously be some kind of upper and lower limit to the houses, schools, roads and hospitals which a country could have, but it might be socially, politically and economically possible to slow down or speed up such building for a generation or so. If a government did this to correct discrepancies between G_w and G_n, full employment could be maintained, provided the problem of the instability of G about G_w could be solved.

In 'Keynesian' terminology, the use of social investment to maintain full employment when G_w exceeds G_n can simply be regarded as the well-known 'Keynesian' policy of public works in a slump. Much social investment is of great importance in any case, and it has to be undertaken sometime. Keynes argued that it was worth undertaking quite useless investment in a slump (such as digging holes and filling them in again) if there was no worthwhile investment to undertake, rather than to allow unemployment to persist.

In terms of Sir Roy Harrod's equations, all expenditure on 'current additions to capital the worthwhileness of which is not deemed to have any immediate relation to current requirements . . . the capital outlay of a long range character, capital outlay which no one expects to see justified or not justified within a fairly short period', is called k, and k is deducted from savings.[1] At the same time, this kind of capital is not included in C_r. Then, if k is 5% of the NNP and S is 12%, (S–k) is 7%, so to maintain full employment, 7% of the NNP has to be invested in ways where the immediate worthwhileness of investment is obvious, i.e., in industry. Then, if C_r is 3, G_w is $\frac{7}{3}$% or $2\frac{1}{3}$%. Thus, provided output grows by $2\frac{1}{3}$% per annum, and this is possible provided G_n is $2\frac{1}{3}$% or

[1] *Towards a Dynamic Economics*, p. 79.

more, the economy can grow at or above G_w. Thus, when k is introduced, Sir Roy's equation for G_w is modified. Before the introduction of k, G_w was $\frac{S}{C_r}\%$, but it is $\frac{S-k}{C_r}\%$ after its introduction. Clearly, if k can be modified, G_w can always be made to equal G_n.

It might be thought that it would be exceedingly difficult in practice for governments to modify k so as to keep G_n and G_w together. However, this is precisely what British governments have attempted to do since 1945 (without, of course, necessarily thinking in Sir Roy Harrod's terms). Social and public investment have been cut back whenever the pressure of demand-induced inflation looked as if it might become serious, while these kinds of investment have been increased substantially whenever unemployment and industrial stagnation appeared to be in the offing.

The rate of profit and its effect on C_r and G_n

So far in this chapter, it has been taken for granted that C_r does not change when the rate of profit changes, and that G_n does not change when the share of investment changes. It was argued in Chapters 1 and 3 that C_r would be higher with a lower rate of profit, and lower with a higher rate of profit. It was also argued in Chapter 1 that a lower rate of profit which raised C_r might also then raise the rate of technical progress. If C_r rose when the rate of profit fell, and the share of investment rose in consequence leading to faster technical progress, investment opportunity would rise, both because of the rise in C_r, and because of the effect of faster technical progress on G_n.

Suppose that G_n is originally 3%, and that C_r is 3 and (S–k) 15% so that G_w (which is $\frac{S-k}{C_r}\%$) is 5%. There would then be persistent unemployment because G_w exceeded G_n. It would be plausible that the rate of profit would then become lower than it is where G_n equals G_w. Suppose that C_r became 4 as a result of the lower rate of profit. Then the share of investment which could be maintained in the long run, $G_n.C_r$, would rise from 9% of the NNP to 12%. Suppose that the share of investment actually rose to 12%, and that this led to faster technical progress which raised G_n from 3% to $3\frac{3}{4}$%. Then investment opportunity would rise to 15%. (S–k) which is 15% would then no longer exceed investment opportunity, and G_w would become $3\frac{3}{4}$% which would no longer exceed G_n. Thus, starting from a situation where G_w was 5% and G_n 3%, a fall in the rate of profit which raised C_r from 3 to 4, and G_n from 3% to $3\frac{3}{4}$% would reduce G_w to $3\frac{3}{4}$% and raise G_n to $3\frac{3}{4}$%. Similarly, the higher rate of profit where G_n exceeds G_w due to consequent inflationary pressure could lead to a sufficient fall in C_r and G_n to bring G_w and G_n together.[1]

There are unfortunately a number of reasons why it is unlikely that G_n and G_w would be brought together in this kind of way. The situation where G_w exceeds G_n with consequent unemployment will be considered first.

Here, the rate of profit would almost certainly be lower than where G_w equals G_n, but it is far from clear that this lower rate of profit would be taken into account in the calculations on which investment decisions are based. It is sometimes argued that entrepreneurs only invest where they can expect to obtain a certain minimum rate of profit with new capital, and that prices are fixed to give *at least* this rate of return with normal capacity working. This rate of return must be sufficient to cover risk and the interest rate, and there may well be a conventional element in the amount entrepreneurs believe they need to obtain.[2] Suppose they believed they needed to obtain 10%. Then, even if the actual rate of profit in the economy fell to 6%, they might still require 10% from new capital, and set prices accordingly. If they did this, the actual 6% profit rate would not affect the technique of production. Alternatively, they might only invest where they could expect to earn enough gross profit in a limited number of years to recover the cost of an investment.[3] Suppose they required this to be recovered in five years. Then, with capital costing £100,000, they would require a gross profit of about £20,000 a year (and a gross profit rate of $\frac{£20,000}{£100,000}$ or 20%), which would allow them to recover their £100,000 in five years. In this case also, a fall in the actual rate of profit earned in the economy would have no effect on the technique of production, because only techniques which could be expected to earn a gross profit rate of at least 20% would be considered. It

[1] See Professor R. M. Solow's, 'A contribution to the theory of economic growth', *Quarterly Journal of Economics*, 1956, and Professor Joan Robinson's, *The Accumulation of Capital*, pp. 404–6.

[2] Cf Professor N. Kaldor's second 'constraint' in his 'Alternative theories of distribution', *Review of Economic Studies*, 1955–6, p. 98.

[3] See the investment assumption in 'A new model of economic growth' by N. Kaldor and J. A. Mirrlees, *Review of Economic Studies*, 1962, p. 178.

might be argued that the profit rate required from new investment would be reduced, or the 'pay-off' period extended when the profit rate which could actually be earned fell. It is far from clear that this would happen.

One difficulty is that firms appear to be reluctant to reduce their dividends when profits fall. For instance, in the U S, net corporate profits averaged $5·3 billion a year in the period 1919–28, and dividends averaged $3·6 billion a year leaving undistributed corporate saving of $1·7 billion. In the subsequent depressed period, 1929–37, corporate profits fell to an average of $0·9 billion a year, but average dividends per annum actually *increased* to $3·9 billion leaving undistributed corporate saving of −$3·0 billion.[1] It is much easier for firms to use their own undistributed profits for investment than to borrow, because much less risk is involved.[2] If dividends fall less than profits when the rate of profit falls, undistributed profits must fall more than profits, and this will make it more difficult for firms to finance investment, which would certainly raise the notional cost of finance. If this happened, the minimum profit rate prospective investment projects were required to earn would almost certainly be raised. Thus a fall in the actual profit rate earned might well be accompanied by a *rise* in the prospective profit rate required from new investment.

A further difficulty is due to the abnormal excess capacity which is probable where G_w exceeds G_n. If entrepreneurs believe that the risk of future excess capacity is high, they will be reluctant to install capital equipment involving heavy overhead charges. Where their capacity to produce exceeds the amount they can sell, and their costs are predominantly labour costs, they can dismiss some of their workers to bring their costs into line with their smaller market. Where their costs are predominantly capital costs, they can only cut them to a very limited extent. If they expect recurrent excess capacity, and they surely would in the conditions where G_w exceeds G_n, they would wish to make the greatest possible part of their costs *escapable* costs, i.e., labour cost, and to reduce inescapable capital costs as much as possible. Since capital with a higher C_r would almost certainly involve a higher ratio of inescapable overhead costs to total costs, they would be reluctant

[1] J. Steindl, *Maturity and Stagnation in American Capitalism*, Blackwell, 1952, p. 116.

[2] See, for instance, Chapter 5 of Professor J. Duesenberry's *Business Cycles and Economic Growth*, McGraw-Hill, 1958.

to raise C_r. Thus, even if the prospective profit rate required from new investment actually fell when G_w exceeded G_n, so that techniques with a higher C_r became the most profitable ones *with normal capacity working*, they might not be chosen because of entrepreneurial anticipation that capital would be worked to less than normal capacity, and techniques with a higher C_r would then be less profitable.

For the above arguments, it had to be assumed that there would actually be lower profits and unemployment where G_w exceeds G_n. It could be argued that inequality between G_w and G_n would never occur because adjustment of C_r through changes in the rate of profit would always be immediate. Starting from a position of equality between G_w and G_n, if (S–k) rose so that G_w rose to exceed G_n, and the rate of profit then fell immediately together with the prospective profit rate required from new capital, leading to an *immediate* rise in C_r; a depressed situation with lack of finance and unwillingness to increase overheads would not have time to set in. This would require immediate adjustment of the required profit rate with new capital to the lower rate of profit when slow adjustment (if there was adjustment at all) would be much more likely, but there is a further reason why rapid adjustment of C_r to a lower rate of profit would be unlikely. In many, or even in most industries, techniques of production with a higher C_r might well not be immediately available. There would be hypothetical capital equipment with a high C_r which it would pay to use when the rate of profit was low, but it would not pay manufacturers to spend money on the design and development of such equipment while the rate of profit was high and there was no market for it. Then, following a fall in the rate of profit, equipment with a high C_r would often need to be designed and developed before the actual C_r could rise. This would take time, and the long period of undercapacity working (in the absence of such equipment) would make entrepreneurs reluctant to buy it when it became available. An immediate change in C_r would then be limited to the industries where there were known methods of production with a high C_r, and they might well be of insufficient aggregate importance to have much effect on the overall capital output ratio.

While the rate of profit is likely to fall immediately after G_w becomes greater than G_n, this would be unlikely to lead to an immediate and significant rise in C_r. If it did not, so that depressed conditions had time to bite, entrepreneurs would be unwilling to increase the share of investment because of lack of internal finance, and reluctance to increase overheads. If, for these reasons, the share of investment did not rise, the rate of technical progress would not rise because faster technical progress would only be induced by a higher share of investment, so there would be little if any rise in long run investment opportunity. Thus, where G_w exceeds G_n, it appears to be most unlikely that the consequently lower rate of profit would actually bring them together and permit full employment.

In the converse situation where G_n exceeds G_w with demand-induced inflation and possibly 'structural' unemployment, it might again be thought that the consequently higher profit rate would lower C_r and G_n. Again, this is far from clear. The forces acting against a fall in C_r are first, the labour scarcity that would be the immediate consequence of demand inflation, and second, the lack of risk associated with boom conditions.

With demand-induced inflation, there are insufficient workers to produce the consumer and investment goods which people and firms wish to buy, so there would almost certainly be overall labour scarcity.[1] With labour scarcity, the cost of an extra worker to a firm exceeds the wage he actually needs to be paid, because the wages of all the workers employed by the firm need to be raised to attract extra workers. For example, a firm might have a labour force of 1,000, and pay a wage of £18 a week, and it might need to pay £18 10s. a week to attract extra workers to increase its labour force to 1,100. Then the extra 100 workers would cost the firm the 100 times £18 10s. they would actually need to be paid, plus the 1,000 times 10s. the original 1,000 workers would have to be paid to bring their wage up to £18 10s. The cost of the 100 extra workers would then work out at £23 10s. each a week. Because the labour supply is less than perfectly elastic, the marginal cost of labour (i.e., the full cost of an extra worker to the firm) exceeds the wage. In deciding on the most profitable technique of production, it is this marginal cost of labour which the firm should take into account; so the high cost of extra labour would work against a switch to techniques of production with a low C_r. With excess demand and labour scarcity, the actual rate of profit might well be

[1] Where there is 'structural' unemployment, there is, of course, no labour scarcity, so the argument in the text cannot apply. It was argued above that 'structural' unemployment would be rare in a developed economy because enough old capital to equip the available labour force would normally be available, and it would be used if demand was sufficient.

high, but the high *marginal* cost of labour might well make techniques of production with a *higher* than normal C_r the most profitable ones to use. Entrepreneurs would probably not think in terms of the marginal cost of labour as such. They might simply believe that it paid them to invest in labour-saving equipment with a higher than normal C_r (where this was available) when labour was scarce. They would need to do this if they believed that more labour simply could not be obtained, so that investment in labour-saving equipment was the only way of increasing output for growing markets.

Further reasons why C_r might well rise rather than fall when G_n exceeds G_w are simply the reasons why it would not rise when G_w exceeds G_n. With high profits, the notional cost of finance would be low. With buoyant markets, there would be less reluctance to incur heavy overheads, etc. C_r would only fall if the effect of the higher rate of profit was greater than the effects of labour scarcity and the confidence that overheads could be covered.

Thus, it is far from clear that C_r would vary sufficiently with the rate of profit (or even in the direction required) to bring G_n and G_w together. Where G_w was greater, a failure in the cost of finance or the profit entrepreneurs require from new investment to fall, lack of confidence that higher overheads would be covered, and possibly even lack of availability of techniques of production with a higher C_r might well prevent C_r from rising. When G_w was greater, labour scarcity, and confidence that high overheads could be covered might well prevent C_r from falling.

In Chapter 3 it was argued that C_r would be low with a high rate of profit, and high with a low rate of profit. The above argument that the rate of profit is unlikely to have this kind of effect on C_r when G_n and G_w differ may therefore appear surprising. There is, however, no inconsistency. Where G_n and G_w differ, factors such as labour scarcity and excess capacity may well have more effect than the rate of profit on the technique of production. Where an economy is out of equilibrium, the profit rate and available technology are not the sole determinants of the technique of production. On the other hand, where two economies with the same technical opportunities for investment grow in equilibrium with G_n and G_w equal, and one has a lower rate of profit than the other, it will also have a higher C_r and higher output per worker. C_r and output per worker in the other economy could be raised if its rate of profit could be reduced, but this is not all. The transition to a lower rate of profit and a higher C_r would need to be managed without excess capacity or other serious disturbances, because otherwise, lack of finance to the individual firm or fear of higher overheads would prevent entrepreneurs from reacting to the lower rate of profit by raising C_r. The difficulties involved in this will be discussed in Chapter 6. It can be concluded here that while a lower profit rate would raise C_r in conditions of equilibrium growth, it might well lower it where equilibrium could not be maintained. Thus, when an economy is out of equilibrium, a high rate of profit might well be associated with a high C_r, and a low rate of profit with a low C_r.[1]

The share of profits in the NNP, and its effect on S

Up to this point in the argument, it has been assumed that S, the proportion of the NNP which people and firms wish to save, is unaffected by the distribution of the NNP between profits and wages and salaries. The proportion of profits saved is likely to be much higher than the proportion of wages and salaries saved. Firms finance a high proportion of their investment with their own undistributed profits to avoid the risk and inconvenience involved in borrowing; so they only distribute part of their profits to shareholders, and the remainder is saved. Shareholders receiving dividends have, on average, higher incomes than wage and salary earners; so the proportion of dividends saved is likely to exceed the proportion of wages and salaries saved. The proportion of profits saved will exceed the proportion of wages and salaries saved, both because 100% of undistributed profits are saved, and because the proportion of dividends (which form the remainder of profits) saved will exceed the proportion of wages and salaries saved. For instance, if 40% of profits are retained by firms, and 25% of the 60% distributed to shareholders is saved, £40 out of profits of £100 would be saved as undistributed profits, and a further £15, i.e., 25% of the remaining £60, would be saved out of dividends. Thus £55 of the £100 would be saved, so the proportion of profits saved, Sp, would be 0·55. This would much exceed the proportion of wages and salaries saved, Sw, which would almost certainly be less than 0·15.

[1] Professor N. Kaldor's assumption that entrepreneurs raise the ratio of capital to turnover when the expected rate of profit rises, i.e., that the capital output ratio is higher when the expected rate of profit is higher, is interesting in this context. See his 'A model of economic growth', *Economic Journal*, 1957, p. 600.

S would then depend very substantially on the share of profits in the NNP, $\frac{P}{Y}$. Saving out of profits as a share of the NNP would be $Sp.\frac{P}{Y}$, and since the share of wages and salaries in the NNP is $\left(1-\frac{P}{Y}\right)$, saving out of wages and salaries would be $Sw.\left(1-\frac{P}{Y}\right)$. S, the overall share of saving in the NNP, which is the sum of these, would then equal $(Sp-Sw)\frac{P}{Y}+Sw$. Suppose Sp was 0·55 and Sw 0·05. Then, if $\frac{P}{Y}$ was 30%, S would be 20%, and if $\frac{P}{Y}$ was 20%, S would be 15%.[1]

Suppose now that Sp was 0·55, Sw 0·05, and $\frac{P}{Y}$ 30% so that S was 20%. If k was 5% and C_r 3, G_w (which is $\frac{S-k}{C_r}\%$) would be 5%. Suppose G_n was $3\frac{1}{3}\%$ so that G_w exceeded G_n. If $\frac{P}{Y}$ fell to 20%, S would fall to 15%, (S$-$k) to 10% and G_w to $3\frac{1}{3}\%$ which would no longer exceed G_n. Thus G_w would cease to exceed G_n if $\frac{P}{Y}$ fell from 30% to 20%. If it could be argued that $\frac{P}{Y}$ would fall sufficiently wherever G_w exceeded G_n, and rise sufficiently wherever G_n exceeded G_w, the change in $\frac{P}{Y}$ would always equate G_n and G_w through its effect on S. There is a superficially plausible argument that this could in fact occur.

Suppose there is just sufficient capital equipment in an economy to equip the available labour force, which is fully employed initially. If G_w then exceeded G_n, G would be likely to become less than G_w which would cause C to exceed C_r, i.e., which would cause excess capacity. Up to now, it has been argued that entrepreneurs would react to this by cutting investment and therefore G, which would consequently fall further below G_w, but there is another perfectly plausible way in which they could react. If

[1] See Professor N. Kaldor's, 'Alternative theories of distribution'.

industry was highly competitive, they could react to excess capacity by cutting prices in relation to wages and other costs, thus increasing the amount they could sell, until their excess capacity was eliminated. They could then continue to expand at rate G_w, provided the rate of profit (which would be reduced by the price cuts) was still acceptable. Provided they always cut prices sufficiently to eliminate any excess capacity, C would never rise above C_r for long, and G would not then fall below G_w. Then the actual growth rate would always be sufficient to absorb full employment saving. Similarly, if G_n exceeded G_w, G would tend to exceed G_w and C would then become less than C_r. Here entrepreneurs would have less capital equipment than they ideally wished to have to produce the amount they could sell. Up to now, it has been argued that they would then raise investment, which would raise G further above G_w, and reduce C further below C_r, thus increasing their shortage of capital. It is equally plausible that they would react by raising prices relatively to wages, which would reduce their markets and remove their shortage of capital by reducing the amount they could sell. If they always raised prices sufficiently where C was less than C_r, C would continuously equal C_r, and G would not exceed G_w. They would then no longer attempt to invest an amount in excess of full employment saving. Thus, with sufficient price flexibility, G would apparently always equal G_w, and full employment saving would be invested, whatever the relationship between G_w and G_n.

What happens here is that wherever G_w exceeds G_n, prices are cut in relation to wages, which reduces $\frac{P}{Y}$ and S in the way outlined earlier, and so accommodates G_w to G_n. Similarly, where G_n exceeds G_w, prices are raised relatively to wages which raises $\frac{P}{Y}$, S, and therefore G_w, and so creates sufficient saving to raise G_w so that it equals G_n. It appears that both the discrepancy between G_w and G_n leading to long run unemployment or inflation, and the instability of G about G_w leading to fluctuations could be removed in this kind of way, if prices were sufficiently flexible to equate C and C_r.[1]

The fundamental cause of long run unemployment or inflation would then be insufficient price flexibility, and not discrepancies between saving and investment opportunity. If there was unemployment, the fault would lie with entrepreneurs who failed to

[1] See Professor N. Kaldor's, 'A model of economic growth', pp. 606–9.

reduce prices when they had excess capacity, because of monopoly power or restrictive practices,[1] or a desire to maintain a given 'costing margin'.[2] The fault might also lie with too high an interest rate,[3] too high a cost of finance,[4] or too high a profit rate required from new investment, because the economy would not be viable (since there would be no investment) if profits were insufficient to allow these rates to be earned with new capital. Prices could not be cut to a point where the profit rate was insufficient to cover interest and risk, or the prospective profit rate new capital was required to earn.

It is immediately evident that even if this theory is correct, it merely attributes the blame for unemployment to lack of price flexibility. Because of the above constraints, it cannot seriously be expected that prices would be sufficiently flexible relatively to wages to equate C and C_r permanently in an actual economy. Thus there would still be divergence between G_n and G_w, and C and C_r, in almost any actual economy, because of these rigidities. There is, however, a weakness in the theory.

It was supposed above that there was initial full employment with just sufficient capital to equip the available labour force. These assumptions were made to give the theory the greatest opportunity of explaining the possible maintenance of full employment. It is also necessary for the theory that profits should be continuously high enough to permit sufficient capital to be worked at a profit to equip the available labour force. There would be a certain *maximum* real wage where profits could be earned with all the capital equipment. If the wage was higher than this, some of the equipment could not be worked at a profit, so entrepreneurs would not be able to offer employment to the whole labour force.[5] Suppose now that the wage was initially only a little below this

[1] Cf M. Kalecki, *A Theory of Economic Dynamics*, Allen and Unwin, 1954.

[2] See P. W. S. Andrews, *Manufacturing Business*, Macmillan, 1949, Chapter 5.

[3] See J. M. Keynes, *The General Theory of Employment, Interest, and Money*.

[4] See Professor R. F. Kahn's, 'Exercises in the analysis of growth', *Oxford Economic Papers*, 1959, p. 154.

[5] It could be assumed that capital, once constructed, required a given number of workers to work it. Then, if the labour force was 20,000,000, the wage would have to be low enough to allow items of equipment requiring 20,000,000 workers to be worked at a profit. Alternatively, it could be assumed that more workers could be added to given equipment, but that their marginal products would diminish. Again, there would be a *maximum* real wage at which 20,000,000 workers could be employed at a profit with a particular capital stock.

maximum. If G_w then exceeded G_n, there would be danger that the price cutting necessary to correct this would push the real wage above the *maximum* wage compatible with full employment. To avoid this possibility, it would be necessary to assume that the wage was initially substantially below the *maximum* wage compatible with full employment. There would then, however, be a different kind of difficulty. In the first year after the initial position, there would be some investment, so at the end of the year, there might be more than enough capital to equip the available labour force. If the wage was initially substantially below the maximum wage compatible with full employment, it would still be profitable to work all the equipment that was potentially profitable in the initial situation, while the new equipment available as a result of the year's investment would be workable in addition. Consequently, at that wage, entrepreneurs could make a profit by working all the original equipment, plus the new equipment. Entrepreneurs employing workers with old equipment would be under no pressure to dismiss them, so only new workers coming on to the labour market for the first time would be available to work the new equipment. If these were insufficient, entrepreneurs owning new equipment would be unable to find enough workers for it unless they raised wages in relation to prices to force entrepreneurs with old equipment to cease employing some of their workers. They would have to raise wages in this way *whenever the wage was less than the maximum wage compatible with full employment* to eliminate labour scarcity.

It is then evident that with given imperfections in competition, there would always be only one real wage and one unique relationship between prices and money wages in the economy as a whole where there would be neither unemployment, nor labour scarcity. If, at any time, the wage was lower than this, (i.e., lower than the *maximum* wage above), it would be profitable to use more equipment than could be worked by the available labour force; so there would be labour scarcity and 'wage drift'. If the wage was higher at any time, it would be unprofitable to employ the whole labour force. At any time there would then be only one relationship between prices and money wages where full employment could be maintained without labour scarcity.[1]

[1] See my 'A theory of Investment, Distribution, and Employment', *Oxford Economic Papers*, 1965, and Professor A. K. Sen's 'Neo-Classical and Neo-Keynesian theories of Distribution', *Economic Record*, 1963, for fuller accounts of the above argument.

Because of this, full employment without labour scarcity cannot be maintained through price flexibility. If, at one point in time, the wage was just right for full employment without labour scarcity, and G then fell below G_w, only price cutting could prevent C from rising above C_r with consequent further reductions in G and employment. But any price cutting would raise the real wage, and make part of the capital stock unworkable at a profit so that full employment could not be maintained. If, on the other hand, the wage was below this initially, so that price cutting was compatible with full employment, subsequent investment would almost certainly lead to labour scarcity because entrepreneurs would find it profitable to work their old capital as well as any new capital at that low wage, and there would be insufficient workers for this.

It may be worthwhile to relate the argument that full employment without labour scarcity is only possible at one real wage to the original argument in terms of G_w and G_n. At full employment without labour scarcity, and with given imperfections in competition, there will be a particular relationship between prices and wages, and therefore a particular share of profits $\frac{P'}{Y'}$. With that share of profits, S, the share of saving in the NNP would be $(Sp-Sw)\frac{P'}{Y'}+Sw$. G_w at full employment without labour scarcity (which is $\frac{S-k_o}{C_r}\%$) could only then be

$$\frac{(Sp-Sw)\frac{P'}{Y'}+Sw-k_o}{C_r}\%.$$

This might, of course, differ from G_n. If it exceeded G_n, it would fall if $\frac{P}{Y}$ fell, but $\frac{P}{Y}$ would then become less than $\frac{P'}{Y'}$, and the real wage would then be too high to permit enough capital equipment to be worked for full employment. If G_n was excessive, G_w would rise if $\frac{P}{Y}$ rose, but $\frac{P}{Y}$ would then become higher than $\frac{P'}{Y'}$ with consequent labour scarcity. Then $\frac{(Sp-Sw)\frac{P'}{Y'}+Sw-k_o}{C_r}\%$ is the only value G_w can have at full employment equilibrium, and only this growth rate (which will differ from G_n apart from a fluke) would permit the continuous maintenance of full employment. The assumption that different proportions of wages and profits are saved then simply leads to the substitution of $(Sp-Sw)\frac{P'}{Y'}+Sw$ for S, and this is no more flexible than S if there is a unique $\frac{P'}{Y'}$ at full employment when imperfections in competition are given.

Conclusion

On the one hand, investment opportunity in any period of time is limited by the technical opportunity for investment. As James Maitland, 8th Earl of Lauderdale, wrote in 1804:

> In every state of society, a certain quantity of capital, proportioned to the existing state of knowledge of mankind, may be usefully and profitably employed in supplanting and performing labour in the course of rearing, giving form to, and circulating the raw materials produced. Man's invention, in the means of supplanting labour, may give scope, in the progress of society, for the employment of an increased quantity; but there must be, at all times, a point determined by the existing state of knowledge in the art of supplanting and performing labour with capital, beyond which capital cannot profitably be increased, and beyond which it will not naturally increase; because the quantity, when it exceeds that point, must increase in proportion to the demand for it, and its value must of consequence diminish in such a manner, as effectually to check its agumentation.[1]

The rate at which 'Man's invention, in . . . supplanting labour . . .' allows output to rise helps to determine G_n, the maximum growth rate which can be sustained in the long run, or (t+p)%, and capital 'will not naturally increase' at a rate faster than this. $G_n.C_r$ is the share of investment in the NNP when capital increases at this rate, and this share of investment cannot be exceeded in the long run.

On the other hand, at full employment, people and firms will wish to save a proportion S, (or $(Sp-Sw)\frac{P'}{Y'}+Sw$) of the NNP. Investment will only be sufficient to absorb this full employment

[1] *An Inquiry into the Nature and Origin of Public Wealth*, 1st edition, Edinburgh and London, 1804, pp. 227–8. (Reprinted by Kelley, New York, 1962.)

saving if the growth rate is $\frac{S-k}{C_r}\%$ (where k is such investment—mainly social—as is not made with a view to immediate profit) or G_w. Full employment saving cannot be made use of in the long run if G_n, the growth rate which can be maintained, is less than G_w, and there must then be long run unemployment. If G_n is greater than G_w, full employment saving will be insufficient to realise the growth potential of the economy, with consequent inflation or 'structural' unemployment.

Since many saving decisions are not directly related to investment opportunity, G_n and G_w will differ apart from a fluke. Nor is there any real hope that C_r or S will alter naturally to equate them. A prerequisite for continuous growth at full employment without labour scarcity is then that the government will equate G_n and G_w by altering k through changes in social investment, or by altering S through the budget.

5

GOVERNMENT POLICY FOR GROWTH: I

POLICY TO CONTROL THE OVERALL RATE OF INVESTMENT

In Chapters 1, 2 and 3, the various factors influencing the potential growth rate of an economy were analysed. Chapter 4 was concerned with a primary condition necessary for the maintenance of full employment—continuous adjustment of (S–k) to investment opportunity. This chapter and Chapter 6 are concerned with ways in which government policy could be used to realise the growth potential of an economy. This chapter is concerned with policy to control the overall rate of investment in the economy, and Chapter 6 is concerned with policy to influence capital intensity. Consequently the effect of changes in the rate of profit on C_r and the life of capital will not be discussed in this chapter. The term 'overall rate of investment' then refers to total investment with a given rate of profit. Changes in C_r and the life of capital which are due to changes in the rate of profit would also influence total investment, and the effects due to this are incorporated in the argument in Chapter 6.

Technical progress and investment

In Chapter 1 it was argued that entrepreneurs would invest in new capital wherever the cost of production with new capital was expected to be less than the cost of production (excluding capital costs) with their existing capital. It is clearly right that entrepreneurs should invest where they can produce more cheaply with new capital than with old, but if they only invested where they could reduce their costs of production, investment might be insufficient for full employment, because they might only invest in new capital with the same productive capacity as the capital it replaced. If a firm had productive capacity to manufacture 100,000 cars a year and a market for 100,000 cars, and a cheaper way of manufacturing cars was developed, it would have a clear incentive to buy sufficient new low cost plant to allow it to continue manufacturing 100,000 cars a year, but it is much less clear that it would have an incentive to manufacture more cars than before. Similarly, firms manufacturing shirts or steel or radios would have clear incentives to invest to reduce the cost of producing their existing outputs, but technical progress alone would not give them a clear incentive to invest enough to allow them to manufacture more shirts or steel or radios. If, throughout the economy, entrepreneurs always invested to reduce their costs of production, but never invested to increase their productive capacity, the economy's productive capacity would never rise, and total demand (which depends on investment and the *multiplier*[1] which would be constant if S was constant) would not rise. Then both capacity and the total demand for goods would be constant through time, the growth rate would be zero, and entrepreneurs would continue to have no incentive to expand.[2]

It might, however, be thought that entrepreneurs would have incentives to expand their scale of production continuously as a result of technical change, because they could cut their prices relatively to those of other producers when their productions costs fell, thus increasing the amounts they could sell. A producer could then plan to produce 120,000 cars a year in a new factory instead of 100,000, because lower production costs and prices would allow 120,000 cars a year to be sold. The difficulty with this argument is that technical change would occur simultaneously in many

[1] The *Multiplier*, a fundamental 'Keynesian' concept, is explained in detail in Professor Joan Robinson's *Introduction to the Theory of Employment*, Chapter 3.

[2] If entrepreneurs maintain constant productive capacity, and invest wherever they can reduce costs, gross investment will be constant if C_r and the life of capital is constant. Total demand (which is determined by investment and the multiplier, see Keynes, op. cit.) will be constant if gross investment and the *gross* propensity to save are constant (i.e., if S, the *net* share of saving is constant and the share of depreciation in GNP is constant). If demand is constant, decisions to maintain constant productive capacity will prove justified, ex-post. If C_r rose (for instance, as a result of capital using technical progress), or the life of capital fell, gross investment and demand would rise for as long as C_r was rising or the life of capital falling, but, in the absence of such changes, a situation with constant productive capacity and constant demand would be self perpetuating.

industries. The cost of cars would fall with technical change, but so would the cost of shirts and shoes and radios. Car producers could only expect their sales to rise in relation to those of other producers if costs in the car industry fell more rapidly than in other industries, i.e., if technical progress in the car industry was above average. If this was so, sales of cars could be expected to rise because the market for cars would be expected to grow at the expense of markets for other products. A car manufacturer would then be right to invest in plant with successively higher productive capacities. On the other hand, if the car industry had a higher than average rate of technical progress, other industries, perhaps industries making clothing, would have less than average rates of technical progress, and the price of clothes would then rise relatively to other prices, and the market for clothing would fall relatively to other markets. A producer investing in a new factory to produce clothes at lower cost would then expect to reduce his costs more slowly than producers in other industries; so he would expect his market to fall relatively to theirs, and he would then invest in plant with successively lower productive capacities if he did not expect the total market for goods to grow. Thus, any expansion in capacity by firms with faster than average technical progress might well be matched by contractions in capacity by firms with less than average technical progress.

There would, of course, be overall expansion of capacity if firms expected total markets to grow, but that is a completely different possibility which will be considered later in this chapter. In the absence of expectations that markets as a whole would grow, firms would only be certain to expect their sales to grow as a result of cost reduction if they expected their costs to fall by more than the average, and for every firm with costs falling more than the average, there would be others where costs fell by less than the average; so cost reduction would not provide a *necessary* impetus for expansion in productive capacity. This argument is reinforced by the possibility that money wages in an economy might well rise faster than productivity, even if there was substantial unemployment. Then the overall money price level would rise and cost reduction as a result of technical progress would often merely allow a firm to raise its prices less than the general rise in prices. It is certainly not obvious that firms would expect to sell more if they were in any case forced to raise prices because of the annual rise in money wages, but were able to raise their prices less than wages because of reductions in their real costs of production.

In Chapter 1, firms invested wherever they thought they could reduce production costs, and it was assumed that the government would adjust the level of demand so that full employment was always maintained. The above argument suggests that the cost reducing motive for investment would not necessarily be sufficient by itself to maintain sufficient investment for full employment, and that action by the government might often be necessary to reinforce it.

Government action could take the form of a stimulus to cost reducing investment itself. Investment reduces costs if the cost of production with new capital (which includes the cost of the equipment needed) is less than the cost of production (excluding capital costs) with existing capital. A government could obviously increase the number of cost reducing investment projects worth undertaking if it could reduce the cost to firms of new capital equipment. This can be done quite easily through investment incentives of various kinds. The incentives used in the UK before January 1966 were *investment allowances* and *initial allowances*, and of these, the former were much more important than the latter, and they will be explained in detail.

With an investment allowance of 30% (the rate allowed in the UK in 1965 for investment in new plant and machinery), a firm can immediately deduct 30% of the cost of capital equipment from its *taxable profits*, and this 30% is extra to normal depreciation allowances. Then, if it invests in equipment costing £1,000, it need not pay tax on £300 of its profits, and if profits are taxed at 50%, its total tax bill will be reduced by £150 as a result of the allowance. Then the equipment really costs the firm £850 instead of £1,000. It pays £1,000 to the firms producing it, but the total taxes it has to pay are reduced by £150 (provided it has profits it can offset the allowances against), so the cost of the equipment to the firm is £1,000 less £150, or £850. If firms took this into account in their calculations, they would replace old capital with new more quickly, because the cost of new capital would be reduced 15%. With a 20% investment allowance, it would be reduced 10%, and with a 40% allowance, 20%, with profits taxed at 50%.

Investment allowances are only one of many possible kinds of investment incentive, and *cash grants* for investment, the incentive introduced in the UK in 1966 are an alternative. With cash grants for investment of 20%, the rate generally allowed in the UK in 1966 for investment in new plant and machinery in manufacturing industry, the government pays a firm 20% of the cost of new equipment purchased, and this reduces the cost of capital equipment

20% with any rate of tax, and for all firms, whether they pay tax or not. With profits taxed at 50%, an investment grant of 20% and an investment allowance of 40% would each reduce the cost of new capital equipment 20% to a firm paying tax, but if profits taxation was increased to 60% or reduced to 40%, the investment allowance would reduce the cost of equipment 24% or 16% instead of 20%, while the cash grant would still reduce it 20%. Thus cash grants and investment allowances both reduce the cost of new capital equipment to firms purchasing it, and cash grants do this more simply and directly than investment allowances.

Suppose there was initially no investment incentive, and that the government wished to stimulate investment. It might then introduce an incentive which reduced the cost of new capital equipment to firms by 15%, i.e., a cash grant of 15% or an investment allowance of 30% with profits taxed at 50%. Suppose that before the introduction of the investment incentive, it paid to replace capital when it was twenty-five years old, and that it paid to replace when capital was twenty-three years old after its introduction. Then, in the year immediately following its introduction, entrepreneurs would wish to replace their twenty-four and twenty-three year old capital with new capital with the same productive capacity, as well as their twenty-five year old capital. They would therefore wish to spend about three times as much on cost reducing investment in new plant in that year as they spent in the previous year. They would probably be unable to afford to increase their cost reducing investment by 200%, but there would be a substantial increase in gross investment in the following years as they reduced the life of their capital to twenty-three years, and through the *multiplier*, a substantial increase in demand. However, once all the capital which was more than twenty-two years old was replaced with new, an investment incentive which reduced the cost of capital equipment 15% would stimulate investment no further. If there were no other forces leading to expansion, entrepreneurs might well return to simply replacing their capital with new capital with the same productive capacity when it became twenty-three years old. Then, unless the government enlarged the investment incentives, so that the cost of new equipment was reduced 20% instead of 15%, growth would cease, although the level of output reached would be higher than it was before the original investment incentives were introduced.

Thus, changes in the rates of investment incentive could have a great effect on the total amount of investment, but investment incentives would only induce continuous growth in investment, capacity, and output, unaided by other means, if they were increased periodically. The same would apply to any other government measure to reduce costs of production with new capital.

However, since investment incentives have a powerful effect on the life of capital and the technique of production, the government might well wish to set and maintain them at the level appropriate to the technique of production and life of capital it wished to maintain. If this required that the cost of new capital equipment to entrepreneurs should be reduced by, for instance, 15%, it would be disadvantageous to raise incentives to stimulate expansion, or to cut them to reduce the rate of expansion, if this could be achieved by other means. If the government extended incentives so that the cost of new equipment was reduced 20% instead of 15% to stimulate investment, the technique of production would become more capitally intensive, and the life of capital shorter than the government thought ideal. If it cut them so that the cost of new equipment was reduced only 10% to curtail investment, the life of capital would become longer and capital intensity less than ideal. If, in spite of this possible conflict with other aims, a government wished to promote expansion exclusively through investment incentives, it would need to make them so high eventually that their effect would be absurd.[1]

Thus, to sum up, investment to reduce costs of production might well be insufficient by itself to allow the economy to grow at its potential rate. If investment incentives were used to stimulate extra cost reducing investment, they might need to be increased continuously, and their use to control the *rate* of investment would prevent them from being used as part of government policy (which will be discussed in detail in Chapter 6) to influence capital intensity. It would obviously be ideal if expansion and the overall rate of investment could be controlled by other means.

[1] The NEDC has pointed out in its *Investment Appraisal*, HMSO, 1965, that with the 30% investment allowance then current in the UK for investment in plant and machinery, investment in plant with a life of 15 years which yielded 4½% before tax, would yield 7% after taxes and allowances. With larger incentives than this, there is danger that investment which yielded virtually nothing before tax, and therefore contributed virtually nothing to growth, would have an adequate after tax return. There is even danger of this with an incentive which reduces the cost of equipment 15%, where the life of capital is short. An investment with a one year life which yielded −5% before tax, and so reduced growth, would yield +10% after taxes and allowances.

Overcapacity working and investment

In Chapter 4, it was argued that there would be circumstances where investment would be sufficient for full employment without the necessity for government stimulation. Where G exceeded G_w, C, the actual capital coefficient, became less than C_r, the desired capital coefficient, and it then appeared plausible that entrepreneurs would *expand more quickly than before* because they had less capital than they ideally wished to have. Suppose the economy was initially in a situation where the relationship between productive capacity and output was exactly that desired by entrepreneurs. If entrepreneurs then started to expand at a rate which exceeded G_w, they would find at the end of a year that they had less capital than they then wished to have. They would then, of their own accord, expand more quickly than before, and their clear motive for doing so would be that they had less capital than they wished to have. Their motive for expansion would be a faster rise in demand then in capacity to meet it. All that would be needed for this would be an initial expansion in output at a rate exceeding G_w. Of course, without government intervention, there is no reason why this initial expansion at a rate faster than G_w should ever take place, but a government could easily bring it about. The government could reduce (S–k), making it negative if necessary, so that G_w was less than the rate at which output was expanding. If, for instance, output was rising by 1% per annum, the government could reduce (S–k) to zero so that G_w was zero. Then entrepreneurs' efforts to expand by 1% would cause C to become less than C_r, and they would then attempt to expand by more than 1% in the next period. The government could then raise (S–k) and therefore G_w, provided it always ensured that G_w was less than G. Once (S–k) reached the level which would be maintained by people and firms without government intervention, the government could cease to manipulate saving and social investment, provided G was then higher than G_w. A growth rate faster than the G_w appropriate to that (S–k) would then apparently be maintained by entrepreneurs without the need for further intervention.

In ensuring that (S–k) was initially low enough for G to exceed G_w, the government would have two possible lines of policy. It could simply cut taxes to reduce S, and then gradually raise them as entrepreneurs raised G; or it could increase its own investment expenditure by increasing k. With a zero G in the absence of government intervention, G_w would need to be made negative, and this would require heavy government investment making k exceed S, (S–k) negative, and G_w negative. By either reducing S or raising k, a government could always make G exceed G_w, and this should always lead to an increasing rate of expansion by entrepreneurs.

There is, however, one preliminary difficulty. It was assumed above that the relationship between productive capacity and output was initially exactly that desired by entrepreneurs. Thus a G in excess of G_w *immediately* caused entrepreneurs to become short of capital. If entrepreneurs had, say, 10% more productive capacity to start with than they ideally wished to have, output would need to rise 10% more than capacity before they became short of capital and were prepared to expand more quickly of their own accord, i.e., to expand at a more than zero rate if overcapacity working was the only factor making them wish to expand. If entrepreneurs had more productive capacity than they wished to start with, the government would need to raise demand (possibly through increases in public investment which would have a *multiplier* effect on demand and output) to eliminate their excess capacity before further expansion at a rate exceeding G_w caused entrepreneurs to expand of their own accord.[1] After the government raised demand, full employment would be maintained provided there was sufficient

[1] It is important to emphasise that if C_r is thought of as 'the amount of capital entrepreneurs wish to use to produce a unit of output', C_r exceeding C would not necessarily make them short of capital. Suppose productive capacity was initially 100 and output 90, and that C_r was 3 and C $1\frac{1}{2}$. A rise in output by a unit would then raise output to 91, and capacity by half the amount entrepreneurs would wish to have to produce a unit of output (since C is half of C_r), i.e., by half a unit from 100 to $100\frac{1}{2}$. To have capacity of $100\frac{1}{2}$ to produce 91 would be slightly better than to have productive capacity of 100 to produce 90, but entrepreneurs would be by no means short of capital, and there would be no reason to suppose that they would wish to expand of their own accord until output caught up with capacity. If, to avoid this difficulty, C_r was defined as 'the addition to capital entrepreneurs desired when output rose by a unit', C less than C_r would always make them short of capital, but C_r would lose all connection with the capital output ratio. In the above situation where productive capacity was 100 and output 90, C_r would be -27, i.e., productive capacity would still be excessive by 9 units if output rose by a unit, and if three units of capital were desired to produce a unit of output, 9 units of excessive productive capacity would represent 27 units of excessive capital. In the argument below C_r will be taken to be the amount of capital entrepreneurs wish to use to produce a unit of output, and with this definition of C_r, a C which is less than C_r (because G exceeds G_w) only induces expansion when entrepreneurs have the right amount of capital in relation to output to start with.

capital equipment of a kind to avoid 'structural' unemployment, as there normally would be in a developed economy.[1]

There are still, however, serious further difficulties when expansion is obtained in this kind of way. Suppose G_n was 4%, and that the government wished to maintain a 4% growth rate. If C_r was 2, this would require a share of investment of 8%, and for the share of investment actually to be 8%, (S–k) would need to be 8%. If (S–k) was 8%, G_w (which is $\frac{S-k}{C_r}\%$) would be 4%. However, it has been argued that to persuade entrepreneurs to expand, G would have to exceed the 4% G_w so that C could be less than C_r, and entrepreneurs could be persuaded to continue to expand. Thus G would have to exceed 4% to make entrepreneurs perpetually short of capital. But a G exceeding 4% could not be maintained for long because it would exceed G_n. Consequently G could not be higher than 4% in the long run, so G_w which needs to be less than G to keep entrepreneurs perpetually short of capital would need to be less than 4%, and (S–k) would then need to be less than 8%. Suppose that in consequence, the government maintained (S–k) at 7%, so that G_w was 3½%. G could then exceed G_w because a growth rate exceeding 3½% could be maintained, even in the long run. On the other hand, with an (S–k) of only 7%, the long run growth rate could not be as much as 4%, because 4% growth would require a savings share of 8%. To maintain 4% growth the economy would need to be able to move up a GG line, and this would require sufficient investment to prevent the life of capital from lengthening. With a 4% 'natural' rate, and a C_r of 2, the share of investment needed to prevent the life of capital from lengthening would be 8%, but where the government maintained (S–k) at 7%, the share of investment would be less than 8%, the life of capital would necessarily lengthen, and the economy would necessarily move to lower GG lines which would mean that its growth rate would be less than the 'natural' 4% rate. G, the actual growth rate, would then be less than 4% in the long run, though it would exceed the 3½% G_w because of overcapacity working. The government's dilemma would be that only an (S–k) of 8% would actually provide enough saving for growth at the 'natural' rate, but (S–k) would need to be less than this to keep entrepreneurs perpetually short of capital to persuade them to expand.[2]

[1] See pp. 79–80.

[2] See Sir Roy Harrod's, 'Are monetary and fiscal policies enough?', *Economic Journal*, 1964.

The situation would then be that G would be perpetually higher than G_w, but, at the same time, it would necessarily be less than G_n. Meanwhile, the economy's capital stock would become older, because the government would need to ensure that saving was insufficient to maintain the life of capital.[1]

If it was true that G always had to exceed G_w for expansion, the position would be even more difficult than that suggested by the above argument. That the achieved growth rate of the economy would be less than the potential rate would not be particularly unfortunate because G might be little less than the potential rate. The real difficulty would be that where G exceeded G_w at full employment, there would be demand-induced inflation because planned investment would exceed planned saving at full employment. Keeping G permanently above G_w would then mean that there would be permanent demand inflation. This would mean permanent labour scarcity, and therefore permanent 'wage drift' with consequent price inflation which no Incomes Policy could prevent. Worse still, the current account of the balance of payments would be in almost permanent deficit. With a perpetual shortage of labour and capital, there would be incentives to import capital goods which could otherwise be produced at home, and to divert potentially exportable goods to the home market, whatever the comparative price levels of home produced and foreign goods. In addition, there would be persistent delivery delays because planned investment would generally exceed actual investment. Without rigid import and investment controls, this would be a situation which no government could tolerate for long. Inevitably, after a period where G exceeded G_w, a government would be forced to cause G to fall to correct the balance of payments and to reduce the pace of inflation by removing the labour shortage. This would obviously increase the extent by which the long run growth

[1] It might be thought that after a period of, say, 3¾ growth with a lengthening life of capital, the potential growth rate of the economy could exceed 4% for a time because the economy could then grow faster than the 'natural' rate for a time while it moved back to higher GG lines. Thus, once a lower GG line was reached, G could be set at, say, 4½%, and G_w at 4¼%, and the 4½% growth rate could be achieved because of the opportunity to move back to a higher GG line which allowed temporary growth in excess of G_n. It might be thought that a growth rate averaging 4% could then be achieved in the long run, because the economy could always return to its original GG line. *If* G must exceed G_w in the long run to ensure expansion, the long run G_w must be less than 4% because the average long run G cannot exceed 4%, and there must then be insufficient saving for long run 4% growth.

rate was less than the potential rate. Growth would be less than the economy's potential rate, both because saving would be insufficient for it in the long run, and because growth would need to be halted altogether in certain periods to prevent the balance of payments and price inflation from getting out of hand.

Fortunately the position would not be quite as difficult as this. Consider Table 5.1. In this highly simplified Table, G, the actual growth rate, depends on, and equals, the annual growth in orders by entrepreneurs and traders. It is assumed that each year, entrepreneurs wholesalers and retailers together order the amount they were able to sell in the previous year, plus the amount by which they think their capital is deficient, if they think it is deficient, or minus the amount by which they think their capital is excessive, if they think it is excessive.[1] It is thus assumed that they only expand orders to make good a shortage of capital, and they then expand their orders by the amount they think sufficient to make good the shortage in a year. Thus, if they thought they were 2% short of capital, they would add to their orders of the previous year an amount sufficient to increase their capital by 2%. If C_r was 2, 4% of the National Product would be needed to increase their capital by 2%, so entrepreneurs would add 4% to their previous year's orders and G would be 4%. In formal terms, this means that G, the actual growth rate in orders and therefore in output is assumed to equal the percentage difference between output and capacity multiplied by C_r, i.e., $G=C_r\left(\frac{\text{Output}-\text{Capacity}}{\text{Output}}\right).100\%$. The *actual* increase in capital in the year would depend on (S–k), which is determined by the government. If entrepreneurs require C_r units of fixed and working capital together to produce a unit of output, a total annual investment of (S–k)% of the NNP would increase productive capacity by $\frac{S-k}{C_r}\%$[2] or $G_w\%$ per annum. It is assumed that the economy's potential growth rate, i.e., the 'full natural' rate of growth plus any opportunity for extra growth due to opportunities to move to higher GG lines is 4%, that C_r is 2, and that output exceeds capacity by ½% in year 1.

[1] This is equivalent to Sir Roy Harrod's postulate B on p. 284 of his *Economic Essays*, which was referred to on p. 76.

[2] For simplicity, fixed and working capital are not distinguished in this formula. Both plant and inventories normally need to be increased to raise *productive capacity*, and it is possible that a higher (S–k) will sometimes simply

TABLE 5.1

Year	Output	Productive capacity	(S–k)	Increase in productive capacity = G_w	Increase in output = G = C_r(output − capacity)
1	100	99½	1%	½%	1%
2	101	100	3%	1½%	2%
3	103	101½	5%	2½%	3%
4	106	104	8%	4%	4%
5	110	108	8%	4%	4%

Since output exceeds productive capacity by ½% in year 1, entrepreneurs will expand orders by 1% to make good this shortage; so G will be 1% in year 1. The government can make the growth in productive capacity less than this so that expansion will be faster in year 2. It can control (S–k) and make this 1% so that the growth in productive capacity will be only ½% in year 1. Then output will exceed productive capacity by 1% in year 2, and entrepreneurs will expand orders by 2% to make good this deficiency, so that G will be 2% in year 2. Similarly, the government can raise G to 3% in year 3 and 4% in year 4. Once 4% growth is achieved (in year 4), the government can make (S–k) sufficient for 4% growth in productive capacity, i.e., 8%. Then there will be no further alteration in the gap between output and capacity; so the growth rate will remain 4% in year 5. It can be seen that with the assumption that entrepreneurs expand orders and output at a rate which depends on the percentage by which output exceeds capacity, a position can be reached where output and capacity both grow by 4%, and output exceeds capacity by just the amount needed for 4% expansion (i.e., by 2%).[1] This can be achieved by the

---

result in the accumulation of unwanted inventories for one period without a corresponding increase in plant and capacity. The Tables below are largely concerned with the effect of excessive capital on the growth rate, and this will have a negative effect, whether it takes the form of excessive plant or inventories; so failure to distinguish between fixed and working capital should not make them seriously inaccurate.

[1] A position of this kind would also be reached if entrepreneurs did not wish to expand at exactly the rate given by a desire to make good a shortage of capital in one year, and if output did not expand at exactly the rate given by the growth in orders. It merely needs to be assumed that the rate at which they wish to expand depends in some way on the difference between output and

government through control of (S–k). Through this, it can make G_w less than G for as long as G is less than the economy's potential growth rate. As soon as G becomes as high as the economy's potential growth rate, (i.e., 4% in the conditions assumed), the government can raise (S–k) to the amount needed for growth at that rate, (i.e., to 8% in the conditions assumed), and from that point onwards, output and capacity would both grow at the potential rate. In the earlier argument, G became equal to G_w at this point, and C therefore became equal to C_r, so it appeared that the motive for expansion would be removed if the government then raised (S–k) to 8%. This is incorrect, since making G equal G_w when output exceeds capacity does not remove the motive for expansion. From this point onwards, if G equalled G_w, output and capacity would grow at the same rate, so the excess of output over capacity would be maintained, and the motive to expand would be unchanged from year to year.[1]

The problem of achieving the economy's potential growth rate would still be difficult, even with this modification to the argument. The government needs to make G_w less than G until G rises to the economy's potential growth rate. This is the position in years 1, 2 and 3 in Table 5.1. In those years the government deliberately has to make saving less than planned investment, with consequent demand inflation if there is full employment, wage drift,

---

capacity—if they wished to expand at a rate of 4% per annum when output exceeded capacity by 8%, continuous 4% growth could be maintained once a level of output which exceeded capacity by 8% was achieved. Similarly, it does not need to be assumed that G, the actual rate at which output rises, equals the rate at which orders rise—it merely needs to be assumed that G will exceed G_w when entrepreneurs wish to expand at a rate faster than G_w. With these weaker assumptions, a point would be reached after a period of growth with excess demand where output exceeded capacity by the margin necessary to induce growth by entrepreneurs at the economy's potential growth rate. The more rigid assumptions are made in the text to simplify exposition.

[1] This is another variant of a point noted above (n. 1, p. 105). There, it was pointed out that if there was excess capacity to start with, and C then became less than C_r, entrepreneurs would not become short of capital immediately, because the excess of C_r over C would only mean that their excess capacity was being reduced. A C less than C_r would only make entrepreneurs short of capital and induce expansion once the excess capacity was removed. Similarly, here, where there is too little capacity in relation to output in year 4, a C equal to C_r (or even a C exceeding C_r) would not destroy the motive for expansion, because entrepreneurs would continue to be short of capital until output had fallen relatively to capacity by an amount sufficient to remove the shortage of productive capacity.

price inflation, and balance of payments difficulties. The government would need to resist political pressure to deflate, to avoid bringing expansion to a halt before G rose to the economy's potential growth rate. But it would also need judgement to increase (S–k) by the right amount when G became as high as this. Consider Table 5.2.

TABLE 5.2

Year	Output	Capacity	(S–k)	Increase in capacity	G
3	103	101½	5%	2½%	3%
4	106	104	9%	4½%	4%
5	110	108½	9%	4½%	3%
6	113	113	9%	4½%	0%

Here, instead of raising (S–k) to 8% when G reaches 4%, the government raises it to 9%. This reduces the inflationary pressure in the economy more sharply, but it also reduces the growth rate to 3% in year 5, and more drastically still in year 6 if the 9% (S–k) is maintained. All the good work in raising the growth rate in years 1, 2 and 3 is wasted here, and the price which was paid for growth in those years, namely demand inflation in those years, is thrown away. In some year after 6, there is again likely to be pressure to achieve the economy's potential growth rate, and the process of demand inflation to raise the growth rate to 4% would have to be repeated, with probably more inflation on balance by the time it was achieved a second time, because of the need to repeat demand inflation. This would be avoided with the increase in (S–k) to only 8% in year 4 which was assumed in Table 5.1.

Table 5.3a illustrates another kind of error a government could make.

TABLE 5.3a

Year	Output	Capacity	(S–k)	Increase in capacity	G
3	103	101½	5%	2½%	3%
4	106	104	7%	3½%	4%
5	110	107½	9%	4½%	5%
6	115	112	11%	5½%	6%

Here, the government has failed to stabilise the boom in year 4, by increasing (S–k) to 8%, the percentage needed for 4% growth in productive capacity. Consequently, the excess of output over capacity exceeds 2% in years 5 and 6, and this causes entrepreneurs to try and expand by more than 4% per annum, which they may succeed in doing for a few years. In the meantime, demand inflation will have persisted from years 1 to 6, and it can be supposed that the position will have become intolerable by year 6. Suppose the government aimed to correct the situation in year 7. Table 5.3b illustrates how this could be done.

TABLE 5.3b

Year	Output	Capacity	(S–k)	Increase in capacity	G
7	121	117½	17%	8½%	7%
8a	128	126	8%	4%	4%
8b	128	126	14%	7%	4%
9b	132	133	10%	5%	– 2%

If, in the conditions assumed, the government increased (S–k) to 17% in year 7, and reduced it to 8% in year 8 (as illustrated in 8a), the growth rate of output and capacity would become 4% in year 8, and 4% growth could be maintained from year 8 onwards. On the other hand, it is unlikely that, having increased (S–k) from 11% to 17% in year 7, the government would reduce it to 8% in year 8. It would much more probably continue to deflate for a further year, (particularly after seven years of demand inflation), with an (S–k) of almost 17% in year 8. 8b in Table 5.3b illustrates the effect of this. In 8b it is assumed that (S–k) is reduced from 17% to 14% in year 8, and this increases capacity more than output in year 8 so that the growth rate in year 9 (illustrated in 9b) is –2%. Then a subsequent expansion has to be initiated from depressed conditions, and this will again involve several years of demand inflation. If, as in Table 5.3a, the government allowed the growth rate to exceed 4%, the subsequent contraction would require such fine judgement that a government would almost certainly miscalculate, and might well then bring growth to a halt.

Thus, long run growth would be jeopardised, both if a government brought expansion to a halt too drastically, and if it allowed expansion to become faster than an economy's potential growth rate, by failing to stabilise a boom when this rate of growth was achieved. It has been widely argued that UK governments made such miscalculations in the period 1951–64, with the result that there was more demand inflation in the period than was needed, and less growth than there might have been.[1]

If governments avoided these difficulties, by either stabilising the rate of expansion at the economy's potential growth rate, or by reducing it to this instead of to zero if it became too fast, there would still be possible inconvenience. For 4% expansion per annum, output must permanently exceed capacity by 2% (or by whatever amount is needed to persuade entrepreneurs to expand by 4% per annum with less rigid assumptions). This would mean that overcapacity working would be a permanent characteristic of an economy growing at its potential rate.[2] This might not be particularly inconvenient. Overcapacity working by 2% would simply mean that entrepreneurs would always have 2% less capital than they ideally wished to have to produce current output. They might wish to have capital which could produce 5% more than current output at minimum cost, to give them flexibility and some possibility of expansion if unexpected orders came in. If this was so, 2% overcapacity working would simply mean that they had spare capacity of only 3% instead of the 5% they regarded as ideal. Having only 3% spare capacity instead of 5% would be their motive for expansion, because they would expand to try and maintain a 5% margin of spare capacity. This would clearly cause little inconvenience—it would just mean that the economy would be a little less flexible in switching output between products when demand changed than an economy where the margin of spare capacity entrepreneurs wished for was maintained. On the other hand, if entrepreneurs did not wish to have a margin of spare capacity, a situation where they always had 2% less capacity than

[1] See, for instance, Sir Roy Harrod, *Policy Against Inflation*, Macmillan, 1959; and J. C. R. Dow, *The Management of the British Economy 1945–60*, Cambridge University Press, 1964.

[2] Professor F. W. Paish has argued that a margin of spare capacity must be maintained in an economy if growth is to be maintained without inflation. See his *Studies in an Inflationary Economy*, Macmillan, 1962, Chapter 17. He believes that an economy would grow at its potential rate, in spite of a margin of spare capacity of 5%. It is not clear why he expects entrepreneurs to expand when they have 5% spare capacity, and, since 1945, growth in the UK economy has certainly been zero when the margin of spare capacity was that desired by Professor Paish.

they wanted would mean permanent production in the rising part of firms' cost curves, with costs of production which were consequently a little higher than necessary.

To sum up this part of the argument, expansion can be induced through the adjustment of (S–k), so that entrepreneurs are sufficiently short of capital to persuade them to expand at the economy's potential growth rate. This would involve periods of demand inflation while the growth rate was raised to the potential rate, and the danger of over or under correction of (S–k) with an erratic growth rate, and unnecessarily frequent periods of excess demand. There would also be a possibility that permanent over-capacity working might be needed with loss of flexibility, and slightly higher costs of production than in ideal conditions.

The 'expected' growth rate and its effect on investment

Up to this point in the argument, it has been assumed that entrepreneurs will only wish to expand capacity when output exceeds the amount they would ideally wish to produce with their capital. Suppose it took four years to install capacity in the steel industry. Then, if the demand for steel exceeded the capacity to produce it in 1965, entrepreneurs would take decisions to expand steel capacity in 1965 which would allow the 1965 output to be produced in ideal conditions in 1969. If the demand for steel was higher in 1966, there would be too little capital to produce it, as there was in 1965. Indeed, until 1969, there would be insufficient capacity to produce even the amount of steel demanded in 1965. Because it would take four years to expand steelmaking capacity, the capacity to manufacture steel would always be four years behind demand.

If, on average, in the past, the demand for steel rose by 4% per annum, steel producers might well consider it worthwhile to expand their capacity by 4% per annum in anticipation of future growth in demand. For instance, suppose a firm in the steel industry had the ideal capacity in 1965 to manufacture 1,000,000 tons of steel per annum, and that it had a market for 1,040,000 tons. It could order enough extra capacity to manufacture an extra 40,000 tons per annum (if this was possible), and if it did this, it would have the ideal capacity to manufacture 1,040,000 tons in 1969. On the other hand, if the demand for steel rose by 4% per annum between 1955 and 1965, the firm might well anticipate that the demand for steel would be 16% higher in 1969 than in 1965, i.e., 1,200,000 tons. If it merely ordered a plant extension to increase its capacity by 40,000 tons, it would have capacity of only 1,040,000 tons to meet this anticipated demand. It would then be unable to meet its orders in 1969 without delivery delays, and this might cause some of its customers to buy from other producers, with a consequent fall in its share of the market. Alternatively, it might try to produce 1,200,000 tons with plant designed to produce 1,040,000 tons with consequent high marginal costs, and extreme strain on plant, management, and labour. If the firm was confident that demand would continue to rise by 4% per annum, it would obviously order an extension to its plant in 1965 which would be sufficient to increase its capacity to 1,200,000 tons in 1969.

If the view that future 4% growth would be maintained was widespread, entrepreneurs throughout the economy would increase their capacity by 4% per annum (on average), in anticipation of overall growth in demand at that rate. They would expand by more than this if they were short of capacity to start with, and less if they had excess capacity to start with, but there would be basic expansion, and the influence of excess capacity or over-capacity working would be extra to this.

Of course, there would be many industries where the gestation period (i.e., the interval between ordering plant and bringing it into use) was less than four years, and if the gestation period was very short, there would be no need to anticipate future growth in demand. On the other hand, the gestation period in manufacturing industry would rarely be less than eighteen months, so firms would almost always have some incentive to anticipate future growth in demand by investing in advance of it.

TABLE 5.4

Year	Output	Capacity	(S–k)	Increase in capacity	$G = 3\% + (\text{output} - \text{capacity})C_r$
1	100	100	5%	$2\frac{1}{2}\%$	3%
2	103	$102\frac{1}{2}$	8%	4%	4%
3	107	$106\frac{1}{2}$	8%	4%	4%

If the expected growth rate of demand has this kind of effect on investment, the problem of achieving expansion at the economy's potential growth rate is much simplified. In Table 5.4 the expected growth rate of demand is 3% per annum, and the economy's potential growth rate is 4% as before. Entrepreneurs expand orders by 3% each year, plus the amount they think will be needed to correct differences between output and productive capacity in the year. Thus G will be $3\%+C_r\left(\frac{\text{output}-\text{capacity}}{\text{output}}\right).100\%$, while capacity will increase at rate G_w which will depend on the actual (S–k).

Here, excess demand is only needed in year 1 to achieve 4% growth, and a 4% growth rate can be maintained from year 2 onwards provided (S–k) is maintained at 8%, the amount needed for 4% growth in capacity, from that point onwards. Output will then be maintained ½% above capacity which will induce the extra 1% growth in orders which is needed for 4% growth in output. Thus, here, 4% growth can be achieved more easily, and a smaller shortage of capacity is needed to maintain it.

If entrepreneurs expected demand to grow by 5% per annum while output could only be increased 4%, output would have to be maintained ½% below capacity to persuade them to expand by only 4% when they expected demand to grow by 5% per annum. Once 4% growth was maintained for a few years, entrepreneurs would very probably revise their expectations and expect 4% growth in the future, even though they originally expected 3% or 5% growth. Then, after a period of stable growth at the potential rate, output could be made equal to capacity, and they would continue to expand by 4% per annum for as long as output and capacity were kept in line with each other.

An expectation of growing demand by entrepreneurs makes the problem of achieving growth at the economy's potential rate so much simpler that governments should do everything in their power to give entrepreneurs reason to form expectations of this kind. For this, it is essential that steady and continuous growth should be maintained. To the extent that it is, entrepreneurs would pay more and more attention to expectations about the long run behaviour of the economy, and less to short run discrepancies between output and capacity, with the result that it would become continuously easier to maintain steady growth, while the need for excess demand to stimulate growth would become less.[1]

It might then be worthwhile to incur a certain amount of short term inconvenience (in the form of inflation and balance of

[1] See Professor Joan Robinson's, 'The model of an expanding economy', *Economic Journal*, 1952, pp. 52–3.

payments difficulties) while entrepreneurs became convinced that steady growth of demand and output would be maintained by the government.

Finance and investment

Up to this point in the chapter the availability of finance has been presumed to have no effect on investment and the rate of expansion. It has been argued that entrepreneurs invest to reduce costs of production with their existing outputs wherever this is possible, that they expand capacity wherever it is less than the ideal amount needed to produce current output, and that they expand in addition to this at the rate they expect their markets to grow. This implied that they could always obtain sufficient finance for such investment.

They would not obviously invest more if they could obtain more finance. It is always possible for a firm to buy shares in other companies, or even government bonds. It has been shown that the annual rate of return on UK ordinary shares which moved with the *Financial Times* index was 7·9% after tax (when dividends and capital gains were taken into account) between 1919 and 1939, and 10% between 1946 and 1963.[1] A rate of return of 8–10% after tax is very similar to the rate of return which can be obtained from investment in plant and machinery, and firms which bought ordinary shares rather than plant and capital equipment in the past will have lost little by doing so. There are further advantages from buying shares in other companies apart from this 8–10% after tax return. It is possible to buy shares in companies making similar products, and this may allow a firm to obtain some control over the pricing and investment decisions of competitors. Shares can also be bought in companies producing machinery or raw materials which a firm needs, or in companies controlling shops through which it can sell. This would help to ensure supplies of materials and machinery (to its own specifications) when these were scarce, and the control of distributive outlets would have obvious advantages. Thus, the overall return from the purchase of ordinary shares would often exceed the 8–10% in immediate dividends and capital gains they would be likely to bring in. Clearly, a company would have no incentive to use spare finance for investment in plant and machinery when this was not expected to reduce costs, or provide capacity for a likely market, when the alternative of buying shares in other companies is so attractive.

[1] See A. J. Merrett and A. Sykes, 'Incomes policy and Company profitability', *District Bank Review*, 1963.

Of course, where the firms in an economy have several hundred million pounds of undistributed profits which they do not wish to use for investment in plant and machinery, and use it to buy shares, the prices of shares would rise substantially, and this would make it easier and cheaper for other companies to obtain equity finance. Thus, massive share buying would make finance easier and cheaper for firms which needed it, but this would not increase investment in a situation where all companies had more potential finance than they needed.[1]

On the other hand, the availability of finance would have a significant effect on investment where finance was insufficient for all the cost reducing and expansionist investment firms wished to undertake. Firms are always free to use their undistributed profits for investment, but there are likely to be limits to the amount they would think it wise to borrow on fixed interest terms, because such borrowing involves the risk that creditors could obtain control of the company if profits were ever insufficient to pay interest on the accumulated debt. A company might consider that there was a safe ratio of debt to its self-owned assets which it was dangerous to exceed. Since undistributed profits increase its self-owned assets without increasing debt, a company with undistributed profits of £1,000,000 which wished to maintain a maximum ratio of debt to self-owned assets of 50:100 would be free to borrow up to £500,000 on fixed interest terms. £1,000,000 of undistributed profits would then allow it to undertake up to £1,500,000 of investment in plant and machinery, and the limit to its investment would be 1·5 times its undistributed profits, if it did not issue ordinary shares. Ordinary share issues are an added complication because shareholders become part owners of a firm rather than creditors, so ordinary share issues like undistributed profits increase a firm's self-owned assets without increasing its debt. It pays a firm to issue ordinary shares, if, at the margin, the earnings yield of the shares is less than the rate of return it expects to earn from investing the money obtained. There will be a limit to the money which can be obtained annually through share issues on these terms, and this will be referred to below as 'favourable ordinary share issues'. Thus, the finance firms could obtain annually without incurring debt would be (undistributed profits after tax+favourable ordinary share issues), and, if the average of the maximum

[1] If share prices rose, the cost of finance would fall, and this would slightly increase investment by making some extra cost reducing investment profitable.

debt: self-owned asset ratio in the economy was $\frac{D}{A}$, the limit set to investment by finance would be (undistributed profits after tax+ favourable ordinary share issues) $\left(1+\frac{D}{A}\right)$. If $\frac{D}{A}$ was determined mainly by entrepreneurial psychology, undistributed profits (which are more important aggregatively than ordinary share issues) would be the main factor determining the amount of finance firms were prepared to use, and control over undistributed profits after tax would be the government's main control over the amount of finance firms wished to use.

Of course, firms might not always be able to obtain as much finance as this, because they might be unable to borrow up to their debt limits. As well as controlling the amount of finance firms *wished to use* through control of the total amount of undistributed profits after tax, the government could make it impossible for them to obtain as much as they wished, through control of the amounts banks and other financial institutions lent. A credit squeeze, for instance, could make it impossible for firms to obtain (undistributed profits after tax+favourable ordinary share issues) $\left(1+\frac{D}{A}\right)$, because the amount of debt the government allowed firms to incur could then be the effective limit on debt finance, rather than $\frac{D}{A}$. Thus, credit control, and control of undistributed profits after tax, are ways in which the government could influence the amount of finance available to firms, and these would affect investment if less finance was available than firms wished to use. In general, a reduction by £100 in the amount firms could borrow would then reduce investment by £100, and a reduction in undistributed profits after tax by £100 might reduce investment by more than £100.

If firms had insufficient finance for both the cost reducing and the capacity increasing investment they wished to undertake, they would have to cut down on one or other of these.[1] It is perhaps

[1] Investment to reduce costs and to expand capacity might often involve the purchase of exactly the same plant and machinery. On the other hand, there would often be cases where expansion only required the purchase of limited kinds of capital equipment, while it was possible to reduce costs by replacing, for instance, foundries, boiler houses, research equipment, computers, without there being any need to invest in these for expansion.

plausible that they would usually give priority to expansion in their productive capacity where markets for their goods were regarded as reasonably certain, and more capacity was needed to produce for those markets. A failure to expand might give potential markets to competitors, and where markets existed for which supply was needed, extra costs due to the postponement of cost reducing investment could generally be passed on to consumers. Thus, a period where finance was insufficient while demand was growing relatively to capacity would be characterised by sufficient investment to increase capacity to produce for those markets, and postponement of cost reducing investment, in so far as this was necessary because of lack of finance. If, subsequently, capacity caught up with output, or exceeded it, firms would no longer need to give priority to capacity extending investment, and they could use their available funds to make good some of the backlog of cost reducing investment which had to be postponed. Where firms had insufficient finance for all the investment they wished to undertake, investment would then fluctuate less than the earlier argument suggested. When capacity exceeded output, investment to extend capacity would be cut severely, but investment to reduce costs would be substituted for it, and total investment would only fall in so far as total finance available became less. Similarly, when output exceeded capacity, investment to extend capacity would be substituted for investment to reduce costs, and total investment would only rise in so far as available finance rose. Since undistributed profits, the main determinant of the finance available, fluctuates less than the relationship between output and capacity where major slumps are avoided, industrial investment fluctuates less than purely accelerationist theories of investment would suggest.

If the government wished to maintain growth at the economy's potential rate, it would want firms to carry out all the cost reducing and capacity extending investment they thought worthwhile. Firms would be unable to do this if they had insufficient finance, and cost reducing investment might then be postponed, with consequent growth at less than the economy's potential rate, and possibly labour scarcity because cost reducing investment is the kind of investment which particularly reduces the amount of labour needed to produce a unit of output. To avoid this, the government would need to refrain from using control over the supply of finance to control investment, and moreover, it would need to ensure that the potential finance available to firms was always sufficient for the investment they wished to carry out. For this, it could attempt to ensure that undistributed profits after tax were always sufficient, by, if necessary, taxing either undistributed or total profits at a low rate. It would also need to ensure that the various financial institutions were able to lend as much as firms wished to borrow.

The effect of this would be to make growth at the economy's potential rate possible, but the stabilising effect on investment of insufficient finance, and the potentially stabilising effect of regulation of the supply of finance by the government would be lost. It would then be particularly important to control investment successfully through the manipulation of (S–k). Since this would be exceedingly difficult, it is possible that use of the supply of finance to stabilise investment could only be dispensed with if entrepreneurs expanded at a steady and sufficient rate because of expectations of growing markets, and that otherwise, fluctuations in investment due to changing relationships between output and capacity would be too severe.

The government's dilemma would be that investment would be insufficient for growth at the economy's potential rate if entrepreneurs were kept short of finance, while if they were not, investment would fluctuate severely when there were discrepancies between the rates of growth of output and productive capacity.

It would obviously be ideal if the overall rate of investment could be controlled without recourse to control of the supply of finance. The government would then be free to use low interest rates to induce entrepreneurs to adopt more capitally intensive techniques of production, and the effect of this as part of government policy to influence capital intensity will be discussed in Chapter 6. If the government needed to control the availability of finance to control the rate of investment, it would often be unable to use low interest rates as part of policy to raise capital intensity, because interest rates would generally need to be high when finance was scarce.

Planning and investment

It might be thought that 'planning' would help to ensure that the overall rate of investment in an economy was sufficient for its potential growth rate. Obviously, if all industries and investment decisions were state controlled, investment could be at whatever rate the state wished. It would then be possible to plan for whatever amount and rate of growth of investment was thought desirable, and, with effective administration, these plans would be implemented. There would then be no need to *persuade* entrepreneurs to expand, and there would be no need to worry about finance; and excess demand would never be needed as an inducement for expansion. Of course, there would be difficulties of many other kinds, but the problems of a completely planned economy are outside the scope of this book.[1]

In the UK and a number of other economies, some industries are nationalised, so investment decisions in a number of industries can be directly controlled by the state. There are moreover planning bodies, the *Department of Economic Affairs* and the *National Economic Development Council* in the UK, and the *Commissariat Général du Plan* in France, which seek to influence investment decisions in industries which are privately controlled. Planning can serve many useful purposes in an economy which is partly privately controlled,[2] and it can certainly be used to help control the overall rate of investment.

It might be thought that control of investment in the nationalised sector of the economy would be of great help in persuading private industry to expand at the desired rate. This is not really the case. The nationalised sector of the economy could be regarded as a sector which did not enter directly into Sir Roy Harrod's equations, which could be taken to refer only to the private sector of the economy. Then, capital in the nationalised industries would not be included in C, growth in nationalised output would not be included in G, and investment in the nationalised industries would be included in k which is deducted from S to determine the saving available for investment in private industry. If investment in the nationalised industries was increased to stimulate expansion by private industry, k would rise, so (S–k) would fall. This would cause the amount private industry wished to invest to rise, because, as was argued in detail above, it would alter the relationship between demand and capacity in private industry. As was argued above, an increase in k would make entrepreneurs in private industry wish to invest more, but, at the same time, it would reduce the saving available for their investment; so it would only raise investment through excess demand and all the disadvantages associated with it. Control over investment decisions in the

[1] See, for instance, Professor P. D. J. Wiles, *The Political Economy of Communism*, for an analysis of some of the problems involved.

[2] See Sir Robert Shone's, 'Problems of planning for economic growth in a mixed economy', *Economic Journal*, 1965.

nationalised sector of the economy would allow private investment to be influenced because it would allow (S–k) to be influenced, but a reduction in income tax which reduced S would influence private investment equally, because this too would reduce (S–k). Consequently, planning through the control of investment in the nationalised industries would add virtually nothing to the means of control available through the budget.

Rather than to seek to control private investment through its control of the nationalised sector of the economy, a government might *influence* it by publishing plans showing the amounts of investment it wished different industries to undertake. It might appear at first sight that these plans would have little influence if there was no machinery for their enforcement. There might, of course, be unsuspected means of enforcement. In France, for instance, firms in certain industries are forbidden to raise prices by law, and planning permission is needed for factory building in the Paris area. They are more likely to obtain permission to build or to raise prices if they co-operate with the Planning Commissariat.[1] Means of forced co-operation of this kind do not exist to the same extent in the UK, and where they do exist, they are not used to control the rate of investment, but unenforceable published plans may nevertheless have considerable influence.

Privately controlled firms need information to help them decide how much they will invest. They have to guess the rate at which total demand will expand, and what a particular rate of expansion of total demand would mean in terms of demand for their products. It would be of use to industry if a planning body made forecasts which commanded respect, and said, for instance, that total demand and output could and would grow at an average rate of 4% per annum in the foreseeable future, and that this would mean that the demand for motor-cars would grow by 8% per annum, for standard lathes by 6% and for shoes by 2%. At first, industry might not take such forecasts into account, and they would then have little effect on investment decisions, but it would take them increasingly into account if they were proved accurate by events, and the achieved growth rate was indeed close to that forecast. If industry was then persuaded to expand, by, for instance, 4% per annum, as a result of published planning forecasts, control of investment through (S–k) would rarely be necessary, and expansion

[1] See P. Bauchet's, *Economic Planning—The French Experience*, Heinemann, 1964, p. 90.

at the economy's potential growth rate could be achieved with little need for periods of excess demand.[1]

The process of working out accurate forecasts of the economy's potential growth rate, and how this would affect different industries would be difficult, but it could be of great value. The planning body would need to have contacts with the various industries to discover how much labour and capital they would need for various possible rates of expansion. It would also need information about the likely rate of expansion of demand for different products when total demand expanded at different rates. For this, price and income elasticities of demand for different products would need to be estimated accurately. The planning authority would also need information about the labour and capital available to private industry as a whole, in the planning period. The various industries' accounts of what was technically feasible, the information about the total resources available, and the information about the relative growth of demand for different products could then be combined, possibly with the help of an input-output matrix to ensure consistency, to determine the economy's potential overall growth rate, and what this would entail for the growth of different industries. The resulting overall growth rate would be compatible with what was regarded as technically feasible by industry, with the overall resources available, and with an input-output matrix for the economy as a whole. The resulting 'plan' would then be technically and economically practicable, provided the information on which it was based was accurate, and that it was internally consistent.[2]

If the government knew, as a result of this kind of plan, that a 4% growth rate was practicable, while a 5% rate was not, it would know that a boom needed to be stabilised once 4% growth was achieved, because a faster rate could not be sustained. It would also know that expansion could safely be stimulated if the growth rate was less than 4%. At the same time, industry would take more and more note of the planning forecasts if they were proved accurate by events.

The problem is basically that 'indicative' planning of the kind described above would only be helpful if it was accurate. If an

[1] See Sir Roy Harrod's, 'Are monetary and fiscal policies enough?', and 'NEDDY and growth: a theoretical question', *The Banker's Magazine*, June 1964.

[2] I am indebted for the argument of this paragraph to an unpublished paper, 'A Method of Planning', which Dr F. Seton wrote in 1964.

economy had a past history of erratic growth, a plan based on the assumption of steady growth would contribute little to the immediate achievement of this, because its forecasts could not be taken seriously. If, however, steady growth was achieved for a few years by other means (such as the correct manipulation of (S–k)), published plans would subsequently have more influence, and this would make the future achievement of steady growth at the economy's potential rate that much simpler.

Of course, published plans promising steady growth might also influence government decisions. The government might feel itself under some obligation to do everything possible to implement its plans, and this might have a significant effect on its decisions when it was also under pressure to do things (such as to deflate to correct a balance of payments deficit) which would cause erratic growth. Without published plans, it would yield to these pressures more often than where it was also committed to the maintenance of steady and continuous growth at a planned rate. The influence of planning and a planning authority on government decisions, rather than on business decisions, might be its main *raison d'être*.

Conclusion

It has been argued that the amount entrepreneurs wish to invest depends on several factors. First, wherever they can reduce costs by doing so, they will wish to replace old capital with new capital having at least the productive capacity of the old. The amount they will wish to invest for this reason, R% of the GNP (less k), will depend mainly on the rate of technical progress. Second, if they have less capital than the amount they regard as ideal to produce current output, they will invest to make good the shortage. If they wish to make good the shortage in a year, they will wish to invest $C_r\left(\frac{\text{output}-\text{capacity}}{\text{output}}\right).100\%$ of the GNP (less k) for this reason. Third, if they expect demand to grow by $G_e\%$ per annum, they will invest $C_r.G_e\%$ of the GNP (less k) to meet this expected growth in demand. The total *gross* amount they will wish to invest will be the sum of these, or

$$\left(R+C_r.G_e+C_r\left(\frac{\text{output}-\text{capacity}}{\text{output}}\right).100\right)\% \text{ of the GNP (less k).}$$

This will be the total amount they will wish to invest. The amount of finance they will be prepared to use will not exceed (undistributed profits after tax+favourable ordinary share issues)

$\left(1+\frac{D}{A}\right)$, and if D is the amount they can borrow on fixed interest terms, the amount of finance they will be able to obtain will be (undistributed profits after tax+favourable ordinary share issues +D). The potential finance they are able to use will be whichever of these is lower.

If the amount they wish to invest exceeds the finance they are able to use, finance will be the effective limitation on investment, and changes in investment will reflect changes in the supply of finance. In figure 5.1, a rise in the schedule DD showing the amount of investment firms wish to undertake from D_1D_1 to D_2D_2 only increases investment from I_1 to I_2, while a fall in the supply of finance from S_1S_1 to S_2S_2 reduces investment from I_1 to I_3.[1]

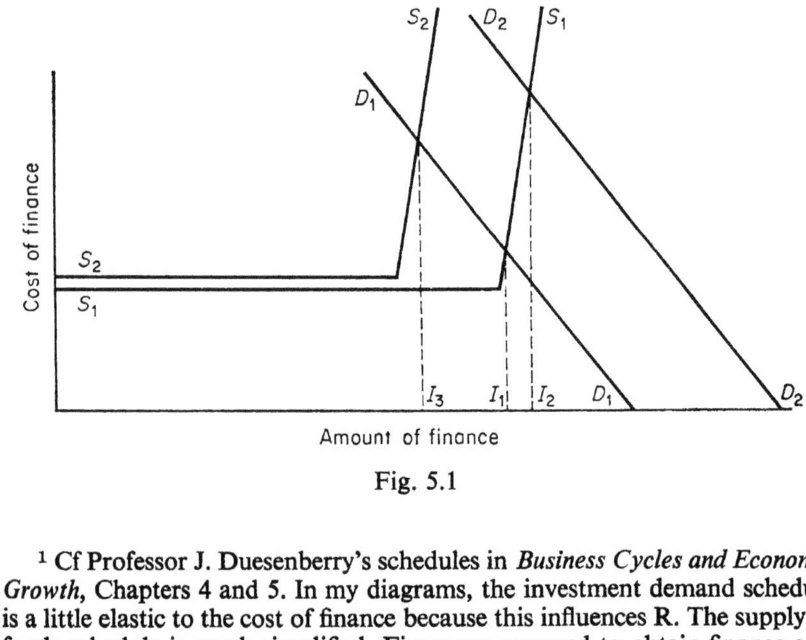

Fig. 5.1

[1] Cf Professor J. Duesenberry's schedules in *Business Cycles and Economic Growth*, Chapters 4 and 5. In my diagrams, the investment demand schedule is a little elastic to the cost of finance because this influences R. The supply of funds schedule is much simplified. Firms are assumed to obtain finance at a fixed notional cost up to debt limits, whether these are determined by the government or their own psychology, and then to obtain extra finance only at prohibitive cost. Duesenberry assumes that the cost of equity and debt finance always exceeds the opportunity cost of using undistributed profits for investment. However, undistributed profits can be used to buy ordinary shares, and it is not clear why the return from buying shares should be more than marginally less than the cost of finance obtained through issuing them. Also, some debt finance can clearly be obtained with complete safety, and at a lower interest rate than 8–10%, so it is not clear why the imputed cost of *all* debt finance should exceed the opportunity cost of reinvesting undistributed profits.

If, on the other hand, the finance they are able to use exceeds the amount they wish to invest, the latter becomes the main determinant of the amount of investment, and changes in investment will reflect changes in the amount entrepreneurs wish to invest. In Figure 5.2, a shift in the supply of finance schedule to S_2S_2 has virtually no effect on investment reducing it only from I_1 to I_3, while a shift in the DD schedule from D_1D_1 to D_2D_2 increases investment from I_1 to I_2.

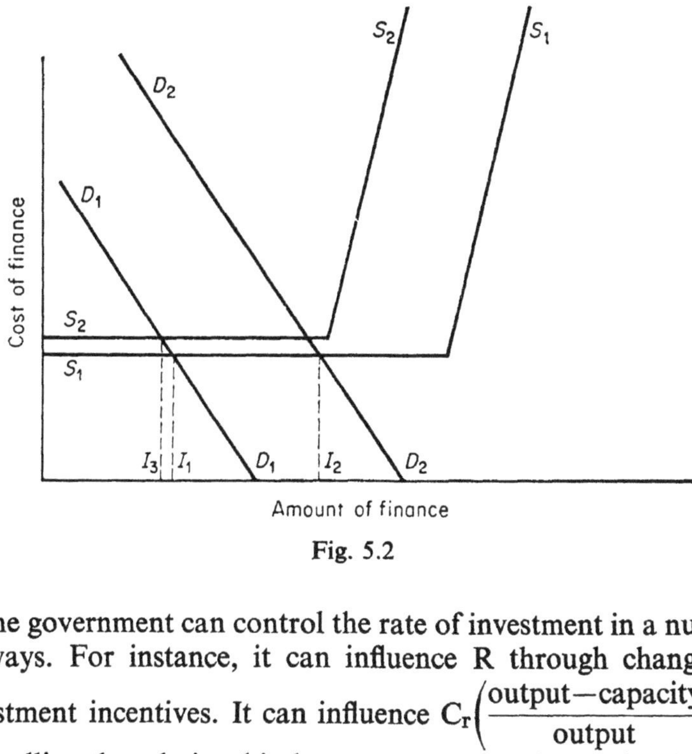

Fig. 5.2

The government can control the rate of investment in a number of ways. For instance, it can influence R through changes in investment incentives. It can influence $C_r\left(\frac{\text{output}-\text{capacity}}{\text{output}}\right)$ by controlling the relationship between output and capacity through control of (S–k). It can influence G_e through 'indicative' planning, and through the growth rate it actually succeeds in maintaining. It can influence the supply of finance by influencing the amount of undistributed profits after tax, and by controlling D through monetary policy.

However, if it influences investment through the supply of finance, any cuts in investment will be partly at the expense of cost reducing investment, and this will prevent the economy from achieving its potential growth rate. Moreover, if the government wished to influence capital intensity (and this will be discussed in Chapter 6) as well as the overall rate of investment, it might wish to refrain from using some of these controls to influence the overall rate of investment. It might wish to fix interest rates, investment incentives, and company taxes, for instance, at rates which would lead to the capital intensity it regarded as ideal. This would mean that it would need to try and control the overall rate of investment by controlling the relationship between output and capacity through (S–k), and by influencing G_e through 'indicative' planning. The nearer G_e could be brought to the economy's potential growth rate, the less would control through (S–k) be needed. The ideal position would be one where entrepreneurs expected future expansion at the economy's potential growth rate, and very limited control would then be needed to keep investment at the rate needed for this. Anything the government could do to maintain growth at that rate for a few years without undue fluctuation would help to give entrepreneurs reason to form those expectations, and once they were formed, the future control of the economy would be much simplified.

It should be emphasised that the argument of this chapter has had no connection with 'trade cycle' theory. In trade cycle theory, it is normally assumed that there is no government intervention, and private saving and investment behaviour and their interactions then, in certain circumstances, lead to cycles in output and employment. Here it is argued that the government tries to control events throughout, and where there are cycles, they are the consequence of miscalculation by the government.[1]

[1] See Dow, op. cit., and S. Brittan's reference to 'Macmillan Cycles' in *The Treasury Under the Tories 1951–64*, Penguin, 1965.

6

GOVERNMENT POLICY FOR GROWTH: II

POLICY TO INFLUENCE CAPITAL INTENSITY[1]

In Chapter 5, C_r and the life of capital (in so far as it depended on the rate of profit) were assumed to be given, and there was then a potential growth rate of the economy. If the policy outlined in that chapter was pursued successfully, that potential growth rate would be achieved. This would ensure that investment in new capital was sufficient to equip new labour coming onto the labour market, and labour made redundant through technical change.[2] It would also ensure that investment would be *only just* sufficient for the economy's potential growth rate; so more than the available labour would not be needed. If investment was more than this, more labour would be needed to work new equipment than became available through new workers and the scrapping of obsolete equipment. In this chapter, it will be supposed that the policy outlined in Chapter 5 is successfully carried out in situations where this is possible, and that investment in new plant is thus

[1] The thought in this chapter has been much influenced by Sir Robert Shone. He first put the proposition to me that entrepreneurs may require an excessive rate of return from new capital, and realise a lower rate with consequent excess capacity. This acknowledgement does not imply that he is necessarily in agreement with the detailed argument of the chapter. The responsibility for this (and for all the errors in the argument) is entirely mine.

[2] Moreover, this would be achieved without any need to work obsolete capital, i.e., capital which is replaced with new in one firm, and then transferred to other firms. As was pointed out in Chapter 4, full employment can often be maintained where the actual growth rate is less than the potential rate, by ensuring that demand and profits are sufficient to permit the profitable working of obsolete capital somewhere in the economy. Where the economy's potential growth rate is maintained however, full employment can be maintained without any need to work obsolete plant, because investment in new plant is sufficient to obviate any need for this.

arranged to be just sufficient to absorb new labour, and labour released through cost reducing investment.

In this chapter, however, a further complication will be introduced. It was suggested in Chapter 4 that investment calculations might be based on the requirement that entrepreneurs would require a minimum prospective rate of profit of, say, R%, from new capital, before they were prepared to invest.[1] They would then set prices (where they had the power to do so) to obtain R% with new plant at normal capacity working.[2] If R became lower, prices would then become lower in relation to wage costs, and a number of effects would follow from this.

First, techniques of production with a high C_r would become more profitable relatively to those with a low C_r, and entrepreneurs would then use techniques of production with a higher C_r. They would, of course, only do this if they expected full employment and full capacity working to continue, but the policy outlined in Chapter 5 should ensure this.

Second, capital would be replaced when it was less old if R became lower, because the imputed cost of production with new capital would fall more than the cost of continuing to use old

[1] If their requirement was that expected profits should be sufficient to allow the cost of capital equipment to be recovered in a given number of years, this would be equivalent to a requirement for a certain *gross* rate of return. For instance, a five year pay-off requirement is equivalent to a *gross* R of 20%, because, with a gross return of 20%, capital cost can be recovered in five years.

[2] Pricing and investment criteria must be interdependent. If R was 15%, and prices were set to give a rate of profit with new plant of 20%, investment would exceed that needed for the production of the goods which could actually be sold at those prices, with the result that the production side of a firm would be willing to produce goods on terms the marketing side would not be prepared to accept from customers. Similarly, if prices were set too low to allow R% to be earned with new plant, investment would be insufficient to meet demand at that price level, and the marketing side would then be prepared to sell goods the production side was unwilling to produce. It is only where prices are fixed to give a return of R% with new plant at normal capacity working that there is consistency between the policies of the production and marketing sides of a firm. Entrepreneurs in industries where risk is exceptional will need to allow for the risk of total failure with some investment projects when they fix their R. They may do this by assuming that the number of years for which they will be able to use their capital will be short on average (to allow for unsuccessful projects with a life of two years or less), and they will then assume that depreciation will be particularly high with the consequence that their R *gross* will much exceed their R *net*, or that their pay-off period will be short (with a consequently high R *gross*).

capital, and because old capital would be squeezed out more quickly because of the lower prices in relation to wage costs which would result with a lower R.

Third, there would very probably be a higher rate of technical progress. The higher C_r and shorter life of capital which would follow from a lower R would both lead to an increased share of investment, and this would very probably lead to faster technical progress, which would raise the share of investment still further.[1]

The economy's potential growth rate would then increase if R became lower. The higher C_r and the shorter life of capital which would follow from a lower R would allow the economy to move to a higher GG line, and the higher rate of technical progress would make this higher GG line steeper, and allow growth to be permanently faster.

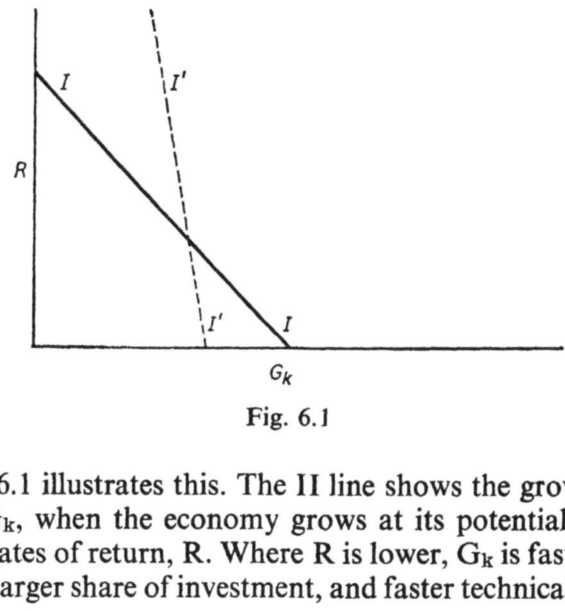

Fig. 6.1

Figure 6.1 illustrates this. The II line shows the growth rate of capital, G_k, when the economy grows at its potential rate, with different rates of return, R. Where R is lower, G_k is faster because there is a larger share of investment, and faster technical progress.[2]

[1] In net terms, the long run share of investment is $C_r(t+p)$. A higher C_r would raise this, and this rise in the share of investment would then raise t which would raise $C_r(t+p)$ further. A lower life of capital would not significantly alter the share of *net* investment, but it would raise the share of depreciation which would lead to a rise in the share of *gross* investment, and a further rise in t.

[2] In the very long run, the II line would be steeper. In the short run, G_k rises when R falls, both because of the opportunity to move to higher GG lines, and because there is faster technical progress on these higher GG lines. In the very long run, the potential growth rate depends entirely on technical

Before the argument proceeds further, another relationship will be brought into the analysis. This requires a return to use of Sp and Sw, the proportions of net profits, and wages and salaries saved. S, which was used in past chapters when the share of saving was referred to, equals $(Sp-Sw)\frac{P'}{Y'}+Sw$ at full employment (without labour scarcity); so a rise in Sp or Sw would raise the full employment S, and a rise in S would imply that Sp or Sw had risen. With these terms, it is tautologically true that r, the actual average realised rate of profit on capital in the economy must equal $\frac{G_k}{Sp-Sw}-\frac{Y}{K}\cdot\frac{Sw}{Sp-Sw}$ (where $\frac{Y}{K}$ is the average output: capital ratio in the economy).[1] Then r rises if G_k rises, and it falls if Sp or Sw rises, i.e., it almost certainly falls if S rises. The rr line is illustrated in figure 6.2 which also includes the II line. r′r′ is the steep line where Sp and Sw are low, and where the actual rate of profit varies greatly with the rate of growth of capital, and r″r″ is the shallower line where Sp and Sw are higher.

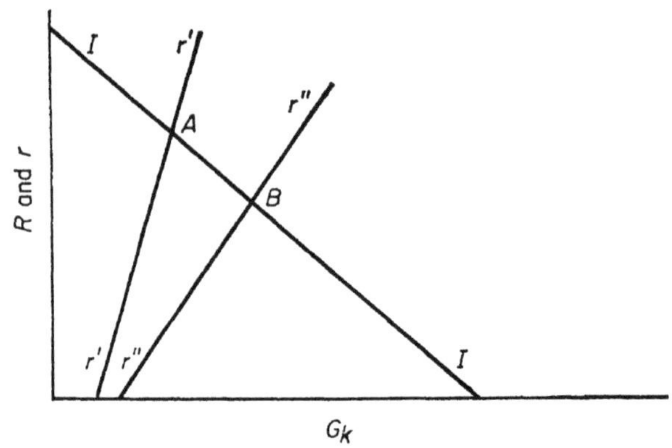

Fig. 6.2

progress, so G_K will only be higher when R is lower to the extent that technical progress is then faster. The I′I′ line in figure 6.1 illustrates this very long run II line. In subsequent diagrams, the shorter run II line will be drawn, but the long run line could be used instead, with slight modification to the argument.

[1] This follows directly from the saving≡investment identity. If total profits are P, wages and salaries are Y–P. Then S≡P.Sp+(Y–P)Sw, so I≡P.Sp+(Y–P)Sw. When both sides are divided by K, the total value of capital in the economy, $\frac{P}{K}\equiv\frac{I}{K}\cdot\frac{1}{Sp-Sw}-\frac{Y}{K}\cdot\frac{Sw}{Sp-Sw}$. Since $\frac{P}{K}$ is r, and $\frac{I}{K}$ is

The rr line shows what the actual rate of profit in an economy must be when G_k, Sp, Sw and $\frac{Y}{K}$ have particular values. Moreover, because the derivation of r from G_k, Sp, Sw and $\frac{Y}{K}$ depends on the saving≡investment identity, it follows that there must always be sufficient saving to finance the G_k given by an rr line.

Suppose now that R, the rate of profit entrepreneurs actually took into account in their pricing and investment decisions was always exactly the same as r, the actual achieved rate of profit. An economy growing at its potential rate would always then be where the II and rr lines cut, because saving would only equal investment where these lines cut. With the low Sp and Sw which cause the rr line to be r′r′, they would cut at A, where the actual rate of profit would be high, and the growth rate low. With the high Sp and Sw responsible for r″r″, they would cut at B where G_k would be higher and r lower.

Indeed, *where entrepreneurs' R is r, the actual rate of profit in the economy*, greater thriftiness, i.e., a higher Sp or Sw, would automatically reduce the rate of profit they actually took into account, which would in turn lead to an increase in C_r and a reduction in the life of capital, and both of these would increase the growth rate of capital. This is simply a variant of neo-classical theory where greater thriftiness results without difficulty in higher investment and a faster rate of growth. If the government wished to raise the potential growth rate by raising C_r, it would simply need to raise the proportion of wages or profits saved. It would not need to take further action to ensure that the saving resulted in extra investment, because the rate of profit would fall automatically to the rate which would allow actual saving at full employment to be invested.

The argument is unfortunately very different where R, the rate of profit entrepreneurs take into account in their investment (and pricing) decisions differs from r, the actual rate of profit in the economy. There are a number of possible theories of how R might be determined in an actual economy.

G_k, $r \equiv \frac{G_k}{Sp-Sw} - \frac{Y}{K} \cdot \frac{Sw}{Sp-Sw}$. See R. F. Kahn, 'Exercises in the analysis of growth', *Oxford Economic Papers*, 1959, pp. 143–5. In the argument that follows, the slight interdependence between r and Y/K in the formula is neglected.

It is possible that R might be entirely conventional. Entrepreneurs might simply 'think of a number' which was independent of the actual rate of profit, the rate of interest, company taxation, etc, and use it in their calculations. The RR line in figure 6.3 showing R at different rates of growth of capital would then be a horizontal straight line at the conventional R—R_cR_c in figure 6.3.

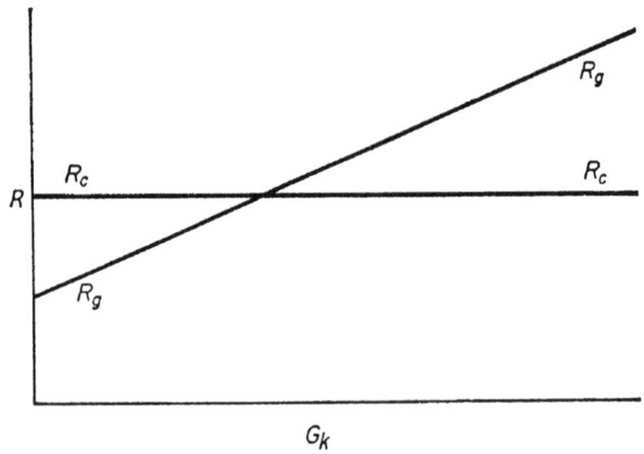

Fig. 6.3

Another possibility is that R might be basically conventional, but a higher R might be needed to obtain a higher G_k. For example, entrepreneurs might require an expected profit rate of 10% when they expanded by 2% per annum, and they might require 15% when they expanded by 5% per annum. The RR line would then be upward sloping—R_gR_g in figure 6.3.

Another possibility is that R might be made up of the interest rate, plus an allowance for risk. Thus, if the interest rate was 6%, and the allowance for risk entrepreneurs required was 5%, R would be 11%. Hence, the RR line would be a horizontal line like R_cR_c, but its height would depend on the interest rate. If the allowance entrepreneurs required for risk increased with the growth rate, the RR line would rise like R_gR_g, its height varying with the interest rate.

It is also possible that R might be a post-tax profit rate entrepreneurs required, and the height of the RR line would then depend on rates of company taxation, and the size of investment incentives.

Finally, it is possible that R might depend on monopoly power. Prices might be fixed to give a particular rate of retuin at normal capacity working, and this would be higher, the greater the monopoly power of the firm. The rate of return required from investment would then reflect this rate of return, and R would be a horizontal line like R_cR_c, its height depending on monopoly power.

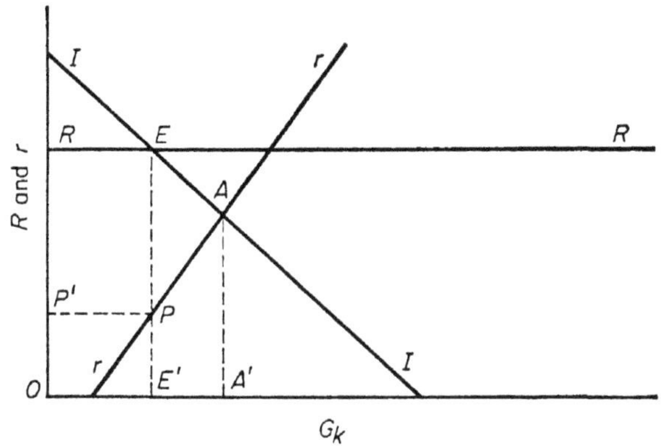

Fig. 6.4

Figure 6.2 showed the interaction of the rr and II lines, and now, in figure 6.4, the RR line is added. In figure 6.4 it cuts these lines above A. It could also cut them below A, and this will be shown in figure 6.5. Since R is the rate of return on which pricing and investment decisions are based, C_r will depend on R, so the growth rate of capital in the economy will depend on R. The growth rate of capital will then be given by the point E where the RR and II lines cut, i.e., G_k at the economy's potential growth rate will be OE′. At this rate of growth of capital, it is tautologically true that r, the actual rate of profit, will be OP′,[1] which must be less than R. The excess of R over the actual r has important implications.

If R exceeds r, the actual rate of return on capital must be less than the one entrepreneurs require from investment, and less than the one prices are fixed to give at normal capacity working. The actual rate of profit cannot be less than R if capital is actually worked at normal capacity. If it is worked at normal capacity, the actual rate of profit earned will be R. It then follows that capital

[1] A rate of growth of capital of OE′ is shown by the vertical dotted line EE′. This cuts the rr line at P, so P shows what r will actually be when the growth rate of capital is OE′. The actual rate of profit is then E′P or OP′. This is the only actual rate of profit where saving will equal the investment needed for a growth rate of capital of OE′—this is ensured by the equation for the rr line.

must be being worked at less than normal capacity where R exceeds r. There must then be excess capacity, and possibly also unemployment where R exceeds r, i.e., where the RR line cuts the II line above A. An alternative way of stating the problem is that where R exceeds r, there must be insufficient effective demand to permit full capacity working.

There would be both unemployment and excess capacity if entrepreneurs employed workers equally efficiently, whatever the proportion of capacity worked. It is, however, possible that entrepreneurs might only reduce their labour force slightly when demand was insufficient for full capacity working. If that was the case, an R exceeding r would act almost entirely on the proportion of capacity utilised, and only partly on employment. While it is uncertain whether an R exceeding r would cause unemployment, it is quite certain that it must involve less than normal working of productive capacity.

It might be thought that the excess capacity would generally be concentrated in an industry's high cost plant, but it is far from clear that this would be so. Where competition is imperfect, and demand is insufficient for full capacity working, firms with high cost plant will have some market for their goods; so firms with low cost plant may well have an insufficient market for normal utilisation of their plant. Thus, where R exceeds r, there will often be some excess capacity with low cost plant, and possibly even with new plant.

It might be thought that entrepreneurs who had excess capacity with low cost plant would then have strong incentives to cut prices and R, to obtain full utilisation of their plant. They could then make substantially higher profits with their plant, fully utilised, than entrepreneurs with high cost plant. If entrepreneurs with low cost plant cut prices when they had excess capacity, R would fall towards r, and the gap between R and r which caused excess capacity would not persist for long. It is, however, far from clear that entrepreneurs having excess capacity with low cost plant would cut prices.

They might base their actual decisions on an R of, say, 18%, which was much higher than r which was, say, 12%, because of convention or a monopoly situation, but even in a competitive situation, there would be a rational explanation for this kind of behaviour. They might know from past experience that, on average, they had been unable to work plant at its designed capacity, and that this had reduced their realised profit rate by, say, one-third, and it is not implausible that they would expect the future to resemble the past in this respect. If they based their calculations and prices on the rate of profit they actually expected to obtain, 12%, and then had the same excess capacity as in the past, they would obtain a rate of profit of only 8%. To allow for expected excess capacity, they would then need to base their prices and calculations on a rate of profit of 18% at designed capacity working, to realise the 12% they actually obtained in the past, and hope to obtain in the future. If they did this, there would actually be excess capacity, cause and effect being interdependent.[1]

Then R exceeding r might cause continuous excess capacity. This would have serious consequences. The II line is drawn on the assumption of growth at the economy's potential growth rate, with just sufficient investment for this. It was argued in Chapter 5 that entrepreneurs could be persuaded to expand at a sufficient rate for this through a desire to make good shortages of capacity. However, if there was persistent excess capacity, they could not be persuaded to expand to make good shortages of capacity. They would carry out some investment because, with technical progress, new plant would become cheaper to operate than old, even though it was likely to be worked with excess capacity. There would then be continuing replacement of old plant with new, the point of replacement being where the total cost of production with new plant (which would include a capital charge high enough to allow for expected excess capacity) was less than the cost of increasing output with existing plant. But cost reducing investment would be unlikely to be sufficient by itself to permit growth at the potential rate. There is then considerable danger that investment would be less than that shown by the II line.

If R exceeded r with consequent excess capacity, there are only limited ways in which investment could be made sufficient for the economy's potential growth rate. It is possible that through 'indicative' planning, or a high expected growth rate, entrepreneurs might expand at the potential rate, in spite of their excess capacity. It is also possible that there might be a number of

[1] Cf the National Economic Development Council's *Investment Appraisal*, p. 13: '. . . if industrialists set high planning rates of return in the expectation that they will not in fact be able to achieve a reasonably high level of production in relation to capacity, they may then, through their pricing policies, create a situation in which the continuance of spare capacity is inevitable and the excess of planning rates over the realised rates is perpetuated in a kind of vicious circle.'

industries where R did not exceed r (because they were more competitive, for instance) and where there was consequently no excess capacity. These industries could then be persuaded to expand at the potential rate in the ways outlined in Chapter 5, and their expansion would increase the markets of the industries with excess capacity, until they too were under pressure to expand. Because of their pricing policies, however, these industries would soon again arrive at a position of excess capacity. Then investment would only correspond erratically to that shown by the II line.

Thus, where R exceeds r, there is likely to be persistent excess capacity, and probably also unemployment. Moreover, it might well be impossible to persuade entrepreneurs to invest enough to realise the economy's potential growth rate.

The government would then have two possible lines of action. It could try to persuade entrepreneurs to reduce R. If the RR line could be lowered so that it passed through A, the gap between R and r, and the consequent excess capacity and possible unemployment would be eliminated, and entrepreneurs could then be persuaded to expand at the economy's potential rate. In addition, the growth rate would rise because G_K would rise from OE′ to OA′. If the high R was due to monopolistic factors, these would need to be eliminated. If R depended at all on the interest rate, profits taxation or investment incentives, reductions in the interest rate of profits taxation, or increased investment incentives could achieve the required effect. If R depended at all on risk, government policy to maintain a steady rate of expansion of demand would reduce risk and therefore R. If none of these lines of action were effective, i.e., if R was entirely conventional, a long-term growth rate of capital exceeding OE′ could not be achieved, and the highest possible G_K would be that appropriate to the conventional R. The only course of action for the government would then be to reduce Sp or Sw (through the budget) to make the rr line steeper. If they did this to a sufficient extent, the rr line would pass through E, r would become as high as R, and capital would grow at rate OE′ without excess capacity or unemployment. OE′ would then be the maximum potential growth rate of the economy, and any attempt to grow faster than this by increasing thriftiness to reduce the profit rate would simply result in excess capacity and possibly unemployment, which might well make it impossible to achieve a growth rate of even OE′. Thus, where convention sets a lower limit to R, an upper limit to the economy's potential growth rate is also set.

The argument here is obviously parallel with that in earlier chapters. Any attempted saving in excess of that needed for this maximum potential growth rate simply results in unemployment or excess capacity, and a lower growth rate than the potential one, as it did in Chapters 4 and 5.

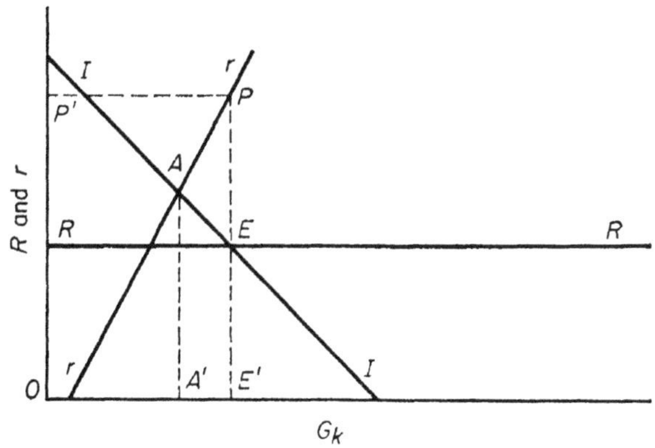

Fig. 6.5

The case where the R R line cuts the II and r r lines above A has just been considered. Equally, it could cut these lines below A, as in figure 6.5. Here, the full employment growth rate of capital is OE′, and at this rate of growth, the actual rate of profit, OP′, exceeds R. Then the rate of profit actually obtainable exceeds the rate prices and investment decisions are based on. Here there must be overcapacity working, or excess demand which prevents a growth rate of OE′ from actually being achieved. The degree of overcapacity working might only be that needed for expansion at the economy's potential rate, but if it exceeded this, entrepreneurs would attempt to expand at a faster rate than the potential rate, so they would try to invest more than the investment shown by the II line, with consequent serious excess demand, price inflation, and balance of payments difficulties.

The government would again have two possible lines of action. If it was desired that the high growth rate of capital of OE′ should be achieved without excess demand and overcapacity working, Sp or Sw would need to be raised (through the budget) to lower the rr line and cause it to pass through E—or, if a certain amount of overcapacity working was needed to persuade entrepreneurs to expand at the potential rate, r would need to be made to exceed R by an amount sufficient to ensure this. Alternatively, if the government was unwilling to raise taxes on consumption, it could eliminate unnecessary overcapacity working and excess demand by causing R to rise through higher interest rates and taxes on profits, or lower investment incentives, if any of these affected R, until A and E corresponded—to the extent needed for expansion. If R was simply conventional, higher taxation to reduce consumption would be the only way in which the excess demand could be eliminated.

Again, there are obvious parallels with the argument of Chapters 4 and 5. If RR passes through E for purely conventional reasons, the C_r appropriate to that R is the only possible one, and OE′ is the only possible potential growth rate of capital. To achieve that rate without excess demand, thriftiness would need to be so regulated that saving at full employment equalled the investment necessary for that growth rate. In Chapters 4 and 5, thriftiness had to balance investment opportunity, or the investment entrepreneurs would actually carry out. In the statement of the problem in this chapter, thriftiness is seen as a factor determining the actual achieved profit rate, and this must be made to correspond to R.

To sum up the argument so far, an economy's potential growth rate will vary with R, and it will be higher when R is lower. To avoid unemployment, excess capacity, or more overcapacity working than is needed for expansion at the potential rate, thriftiness must always be so adjusted that r equals R, or, if overcapacity working is needed for expansion at the potential rate, r must only exceed R by the amount necessary for this degree of overcapacity working.[1] Then, to raise the economy's potential growth rate, R must be lowered. This might be achieved as a result of lower interest rates, lower company taxation, or stronger investment incentives. If policy to lower R was successful, and a

[1] It is suggested here that continuous growth at full employment requires that R correspond to r, and that investment be just sufficient for the potential growth rate where R equals r. It was argued in Chapter 4 that only one share of profits P′/Y′, would be compatible with full employment without labour scarcity at any one time. It may be wondered whether the above conditions are compatible with this share of profits. I have argued that they are in my 'A theory of investment, distribution, and employment', *Oxford Economic Papers*, 1965. It should be noted that both price flexibility leading to correspondence between R and r, and investment just sufficient for the potential growth rate are needed for continuous growth at full employment without labour scarcity. Price flexibility alone is an insufficient condition for this, as I argued in Chapter 4.

higher potential growth rate resulted, greater thriftiness would then be needed to reduce r.

Up to now, ways of eliminating possible discrepancies between R and r which cause excess capacity or excess demand have been considered. It is now time to consider how the analysis relates to policy for maximum growth. Professor Joan Robinson has argued that consumption will be maximised *eventually* where the rate of profit equals the rate growth of capital.[1] The rate of profit equals the rate of growth of capital on the 45° line through the origin in figure 6.6, so consumption would eventually be maximised if the rr and RR lines cut the II line where it cuts the 45° line through the origin, i.e., at M. With this situation, the life of capital and C_r would eventually become most favourable to consumption. It is not implausible that the long-term limit to the growth rate might be 5% or less, and R would then need to be reduced to something like 5%. It is unlikely that this could ever be achieved, but the purpose of public policy could be to make R as low as possible.

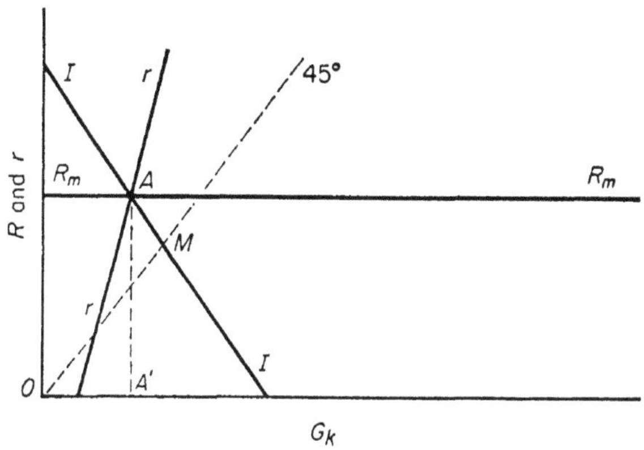

Fig. 6.6

For this, interest rates could be lowered as much as possible, and it would be important to keep them low for some time. If

[1] See Professor Joan Robinson's, 'A neo-classical theorem', *Review of Economic Studies*', 1962. In her theorem, higher investment does not raise the rate of technical progress, so investment leads to less growth than in the present argument. Consequently, in the conditions assumed here, consumption would be maximised eventually where investment was pushed rather further than in her analysis, i.e., where the rate of profit became less than the growth rate. With a 4% growth rate, the R for maximum consumption might then be 3% instead of 4%. Since it would almost certainly be impossible to reduce R below 7% or so, this qualification is entirely academic, and it will be neglected below.

entrepreneurs were to be persuaded that a 7% return, for instance, was sufficient to cover interest and risk, the interest rate would need to be held substantially below 7% for some years. It is only then that they would begin to regard 4%, for instance, as the normal interest rate, and 7% as a rate of return which adequately covered this. An interest rate fluctuating between 4% and 6% would have less effect, because entrepreneurs could not then have confidence that a 7% return would be adequate throughout the life of long-lived capital. This is why the use of low interest rates to raise capital intensity would preclude their use to control investment from year to year.

Reductions in profits taxation might also significantly reduce R. In so far as entrepreneurs set prices and invest to try and obtain a rate of return they regard as adequate *after tax*, lower profits taxation would reduce the return they required *before tax*, and allow them to cut prices in relation to costs. Lower profits taxation might also reduce R by stimulating competition. With profits taxed at 50%, a firm with a cost advantage of £1 a unit over competitors must pay half the extra profit due to this to the government. The stimulus to reduce costs relatively to those of competitors must then be greatly reduced. It would obviously be politically unacceptable for companies to pay no tax, but if company taxes were assessed on the basis of 'pay-roll' or 'value-added',[1] as suggested in Chapter 1, they would keep 100% of any profits due to extra efficiency. Moreover, with a 'pay-roll' tax, investment in new plant requiring the same labour as old would add nothing to a firm's total tax bill, so the entire extra profit due to the investment would go to the firm. A firm might then be prepared to accept a lower return from investment before tax, i.e., a lower R, than it would where about 50% of any extra profit due to cost reducing investment went to the government. It then seems possible that the substitution of 'pay-roll' or 'value-added' taxation for profits taxation might reduce R substantially, both because it might reduce the *before tax* return sought by entrepreneurs from investment, and because it might stimulate competition.[2]

[1] Wage and salary costs form approximately three-quarters of 'value added', so a 'value-added' tax would be three-quarters 'pay-roll' tax.

[2] It is unfortunate that the Richardson Committee (*Committee on Turnover Taxation*, HMSO, Cmnd 2300, March 1964) recommended against the substitution of a 'value-added' tax for profits taxation, in the UK. They believed that a 'value-added' tax would be passed on, while reductions in

Investment incentives for investment in plant and machinery also have a significant effect on the return from investment *after taxation and government grants*. Of course, if 'pay-roll' or 'value-added' taxation was substituted for profits taxation, the incentives would need to reduce a firm's liability for 'pay-roll' or 'value-added' tax instead of profits tax. There would be an ideal rate for investment incentives. Suppose entrepreneurs would not accept a return of less than 7% after taxation and government grants, while the government wished investment in plant and machinery to be pushed to the point where the marginal return from it, i.e., R was 5% before tax. The incentives could then be fixed so that, *with plant and machinery* of normal life, a 7% return after taxation and government grants was equivalent to a 5% before tax return. If incentives were larger, entrepreneurs would push investment in plant and machinery to the point where the return before tax was less than 5%, while if they were lower, the marginal return would exceed 5%. The government could then work out the rate of incentives appropriate to the R for plant and machinery which it wished to maintain. If investment incentives were then maintained at this 'ideal' rate, they would have the ideal long run effect on R, so it would be undesirable to vary them from year to year to control short-run fluctuations in investment if this could be avoided.

R would also be affected by monopolistic and restrictive practices, and the elimination of these would form a significant part of policy to reduce R. It would also be affected by risk, and this would be reduced to the extent that fluctuations in demand became less.

All these measures would have little effect on R if it was *entirely* conventional, though it is unlikely that it would be, since it is improbable that interest rates and taxation have *no* effect on prices and the required return from investment *in the long run*. It is, however, possible that even a purely conventional R could be lowered. If entrepreneurs with low cost plant became aware that too high a required rate of return actually caused their realised

---

profits taxation would not affect prices. With these effects, the substitution of 'value-added' taxation for profits taxation would not lead to a fall in R. The Committee's conclusion is, however, most surprising, because their contention is that low cost producers who would pay less tax altogether after the change-over, would nevertheless raise their prices (as a consequence of a reduction in their total tax bill). It is difficult to believe that this would be the case—particularly in the long run.

profit rates to be lower than they otherwise would be, there might be reductions in the rates they required new capital to earn. It is also possible that they might use methods of investment appraisal which exaggerated the rate of return they believed they needed.[1] Here, anything that could be done to cause more rational methods of investment appraisal, like the 'discounted cash flow'[2] method, to be more widely used would be helpful.

Suppose that R could eventually be reduced to R_m—shown by the R_mR_m line in figure 6.6, through the various policy measures outlined above. It would take time for the various measures to have their full effect on R, so R might only fall to R_m some years after the various changes suggested took place. With R at R_m, OA′ would be the fastest possible growth rate, since R_mR_m cuts the II line at A. To achieve this maximum potential growth rate without excess demand or excess capacity, the rr line would also need to pass through A, as in figure 6.6. Where the II, the R_mR_m and the rr lines all pass through one point, the fastest achievable growth rate is attained, and consumption would eventually be raised to the greatest possible extent, given the difficulties in lowering R.

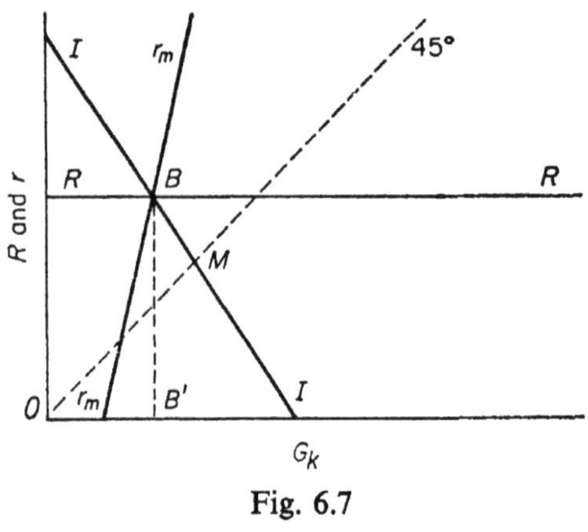

Fig. 6.7

Of course, the factor limiting growth might be unwillingness to save rather than inability to reduce R. There might well be political pressures which would prevent a government from increasing saving, i.e., Sp and Sw, beyond a certain point. If, with

[1] See the NEDC's *Investment Appraisal*, and my 'A theory of investment, distribution, and employment'.

[2] The 'discounted cash flow' method of investment appraisal is explained in the NEDC's *Investment Appraisal*.

maximum saving, the rr line was $r_m r_m$ (in figure 6.7), this would determine the maximum possible growth rate. If $r_m r_m$ cut the II line at B, OB′ would be the maximum possible growth rate, because this would be the fastest growth rate where saving could equal investment. Then the government would need to try to make the RR line pass through B, and for this, it might even need to raise R by raising interest rates, etc. Thus growth might be limited by the $R_m R_m$ line which shows the minimum possible R, or the $r_m r_m$ line which shows maximum practicable saving. Either could set the ultimate limit to growth. The $R_m R_m$ line cuts the II line at A in figure 6.6 and the $r_m r_m$ line cuts it at B in figure 6.7, and the effective limit to growth will then be set by whichever of these is most to the left of M. If A is more to the left of M than B, OA′ will be less than OB′, so possible saving would permit faster growth than the minimum R. Hence the minimum R would effectively limit growth, and the economy's maximum potential saving would not be needed. If B was to the left of A, OB′ would be less than OA′, so the economy's maximum saving would then limit growth.

There is one obvious qualification to the argument. A growth rate of capital of OA′ or OB′ would eventually raise consumption to the greatest practicable extent, but it would reduce consumption in the short run if a higher share of investment was needed to achieve it. It is sometimes argued that a society has a certain rate of time preference, R_t, between present and future consumption. If the rate of return on capital at the margin is R%, an extra £100 of consumption foregone in the present year would permit extra annual consumption of at least £R in all future years. It would permit extra consumption of more than £R in future years to the extent that imperfect competition, economies of scale, and external economies caused the total returns from investment to exceed the returns to the investing firms. If R_t was less than R, all would definitely be well, because even an extra £R_t in perpetuity would then be sufficient compensation for £100 foregone in the present, and the return of at least £R which is actually obtained exceeds this. If, on the other hand, R_t exceeded R, all might not be well because the permanent annual future increase in consumption might be insufficient compensation for £100 foregone in the present. It would then be wrong to reduce R below R_t to a greater extent than that justified by economies of scale, external economies, and imperfections in competition.

Thus, to sum up, if the government wished to increase an economy's potential growth rate, it would need to do everything possible to reduce R, the rate of return sought by entrepreneurs, as *long-term* policy. It would, however, be wrong to reduce it below the R needed to absorb maximum saving. It would also be wrong to reduce it too much below R_t, the community's rate of time preference between present and future consumption. Finally, it would be wrong to reduce it below the growth rate, though this is a highly academic restriction. As Professor Joan Robinson has remarked, '. . . if there is any rough correspondence between reality and the type of analysis here set out, the fact that the rate of profit on capital may be of the order of 15 or 20 per cent in an economy that is growing at the rate of two or three per cent per annum, does suggest some interesting lines of thought'.[1] Where the gap between the profit rate and the growth rate is as large as she suggests, there can be little danger that R could become less than the growth rate in the foreseeable future.

In the short term, the government must, of course, reduce thriftiness, i.e., Sp or Sw, where R exceeds r with consequent excess capacity and possibly unemployment, and increase it where r exceeds R with more overcapacity working than is needed for expansion at the potential rate. This will ensure that saving is always just sufficient to realise the growth potential made possible by changes in R. Naturally, thriftiness should only be increased to eliminate excess demand and unnecessary overcapacity working where entrepreneurs are trying to expand at the potential rate, because temporary excess demand may sometimes be needed (as was argued in Chapter 5) to raise their rate of expansion to the potential rate.

The essential feature of policy to raise the potential growth rate in the long run, by raising capital intensity, is that R must be lowered gradually (to avoid dislocation), and saving increased *as* R is reduced. The difficulty in raising capital intensity is that the lower rate of profit needed to induce higher capital intensity may have the opposite effect of that desired. If a lower rate of profit was simply due to higher saving, entrepreneurs would be unlikely to have the confidence needed to raise their overheads by adopting techniques of production with a higher C_r. They would much more probably cut investment to a minimum. Hence, if a lower profit rate is to raise C_r, it must be acceptable to entrepreneurs, and lower interest rates and profits taxation are probably needed to ensure this. If, for political reasons, a government insisted on

[1] Joan Robinson, 'A neo-classical theorem', p. 224.

taxing profits more heavily than in the past, and insisted on taxing profits rather than 'pay-roll' or 'value-added', it would almost certainly reduce the potential growth rate. It would do this, however much it favoured growth in other ways—that is, if it raised profits taxation and left investment decisions in private hands.

7

GROWTH AND THE BALANCE OF PAYMENTS

The only reference to the balance of payments up to this point in the argument has been the proposition that there is likely to be a deficit in the current account where planned investment exceeds planned saving at full employment. It was argued in Chapter 5 that it might be necessary to have a period of demand inflation with consequent balance of payments difficulties while a country's growth rate was raised to its potential rate, and a country would need to have sufficient reserves (or borrowing power) to meet the deficits due to this, but the question which will now be considered is whether a balance of payments deficit can be avoided once the potential growth rate is achieved. It will therefore be assumed in this chapter that growth is maintained at the potential rate without excess demand—as a result of the successful pursuit of policy outlined in past chapters. The question which then needs to be answered is whether a favourable balance of payments can be maintained at this growth rate. If it cannot, it might be impossible to maintain continuous growth at the potential rate, because current account deficits might prevent the government from allowing it to be maintained.

Initially, it will be assumed that prices and the quality of goods traded are either unchanged at home and abroad, or that home and foreign prices rise at the same rate. It will also be assumed that exports equal imports initially, and that full use is made of productive capacity abroad.[1]

Suppose the foreign income elasticity of demand for goods produced in the home country is E_f, while the home country's

[1] With this assumption, the repercussions of changes in the home country's imports on foreign countries' incomes, and so on their demand for the home country's exports can be ignored, which much simplifies the argument.

income elasticity of demand for foreign goods is E_h. E_f is the

$$\frac{\text{percentage rise in foreign imports of the home country's goods}}{\text{percentage rise in foreign real incomes}},$$

while E_h is the

$$\frac{\text{percentage rise in imports in the home country}}{\text{percentage rise in real incomes in the home country.}}$$

Foreign imports of the home country's goods are, of course, its exports, so E_f is the

$$\frac{\text{percentage rise in the home country's exports}}{\text{percentage rise in foreign real incomes}}.$$

If E_f was 0·5, the home country's exports would grow by 0·5% for every 1% by which foreign incomes grew. If foreign incomes rose 10%, the home country's exports would rise 5%, and if foreign incomes grew by G_f% per annum, the home country's exports would grow by $0{\cdot}5.G_f$% per annum. More generally, the home country's exports grow by $E_f.G_f$% per annum. Similarly, if the home country's income elasticity of demand for imports, E_h, was 0·75, and its growth rate G%, its imports would grow by $0{\cdot}75.G$% per annum, and, more generally, its imports will grow by $E_h.G$% per annum. Thus a country's exports grow by $E_f.G_f$% per annum, and its imports by $E_h.G$% per annum.

If the home country's current account is to remain balanced, exports and imports must grow at the same rate, so $E_f.G_f$ must equal $E_h.G$. If $E_f.G_f$ exceeded $E_h.G$, exports would grow more quickly than imports, and the current account would move increasingly into surplus, while it would move into deficit if $E_h.G$ exceeded $E_f.G_f$. Thus where E_fG_f exceeds $E_h.G$, there is a growing surplus and where $E_h.G$ exceeds $E_f.G_f$, there is a growing deficit. Rearranging the terms, there is a growing surplus where G is less than $G_f.\frac{E_f}{E_h}$, and a growing deficit where G exceeds $G_f.\frac{E_f}{E_h}$. The home country then has a critical growth rate, $\bar{G}$, (equalling $G_f.\frac{E_f}{E_h}$), where its exports and imports grow at the same rate. If its growth rate exceeds $\bar{G}$, imports will rise faster than exports, and its current account will move into deficit, while if its growth rate is less than $\bar{G}$, exports will rise faster than imports, and its current account will move into surplus. Since $\bar{G}=G_f.\frac{E_f}{E_h}$, $\frac{\bar{G}}{G_f}=\frac{E_f}{E_h}$. Thus the ratio of the critical growth rate to foreign growth rates equals the ratio of the foreign income elasticity of demand for the home country's goods to the home country's income elasticity of demand for foreign goods.

$\frac{\bar{G}}{G_f}$ is less than 1 if $\frac{E_f}{E_h}$ is less than 1. This means that the home country's critical growth rate must be less than foreign growth rates if foreigners reduce the proportion of their incomes which they spend on the home country's goods as they become richer, while people in the home country switch their spending towards foreign goods as they become richer. This could happen for two reasons in particular.

First, if manufacturers in the home country designed consumer goods to appeal mainly to people with low incomes, while foreign manufacturers designed goods to appeal to people with higher incomes, the home country's $\frac{E_f}{E_h}$ might well be less than 1, and its critical growth rate therefore less than foreign growth rates. As its real incomes rose, its population would switch purchases more and more towards the foreign goods designed to appeal to people with higher incomes, and foreigners would switch their purchases away from the home country's goods as they became richer.[1]

Second, a country might specialise in the production of goods for which the income elasticity of demand was low. As incomes in a country rise, spending on, for instance, woollen and cotton clothing, beer, bicycles, and standard lathes generally rises less quickly than incomes, while spending on, for instance, cameras, motor-cars, whisky, automatic lathes and clothes made from artificial fibres rises more quickly than incomes. A country specialising in the production of goods of the former kind might then have an $\frac{E_f}{E_h}$ of less than 1, and a critical growth rate which was therefore less than foreign growth rates.[2]

[1] It appears to the author that some UK manufacturers (of, for instance, furniture, furnishings, radios, clothes) design goods with UK consumers with low incomes in mind, while foreign manufacturers (for instance, Scandinavian, Swiss, German) often manage to design and sell goods to the workers in their countries which also appeal to people with higher incomes. Then, as UK workers become richer, they may spend a higher proportion of their incomes on foreign goods, while foreigners in the countries mentioned might spend a higher proportion of their incomes on their own goods as they become richer.

[2] If income elasticities of demand were high at home and abroad for products requiring scientific and engineering skills, a country with inadequate

As $\bar{G}$, the critical growth rate, depends partly on G_f, i.e., on foreign growth rates, $\left(\text{since } \bar{G}=G_f.\frac{E_f}{E_h}\right)$, it is unlikely to be stable, as foreign incomes are unlikely to grow at steady rates. The home country will, however, have a certain $\bar{G}$ at any one time. If this $\bar{G}$ exceeds its potential growth rate, it will be in a most fortunate situation. It will be unable to grow as quickly as $\bar{G}$ in any case, and its exports will grow more quickly than its imports with a growth rate of less than $\bar{G}$, and its current account will be in continuous and increasing surplus. It could then aim to achieve its potential growth rate in the ways outlined in earlier chapters, and its balance of payments would present no obstacle to this.

If, however, a country's potential growth rate exceeded $\bar{G}$, it would be in a most difficult situation. If it succeeded in achieving its potential growth rate, its imports would grow more quickly than its exports, and its current account would move increasingly into deficit. Its government might then be unable to allow it to continue to grow at its potential rate. It might be forced to restrict its growth rate to $\bar{G}$, the fastest growth rate where imports would grow no faster than exports.[1] Then $\bar{G}$ might be the fastest growth rate the country concerned could achieve, and policy to raise its growth rate would then need to centre on policy to raise $\bar{G}$, i.e., on policy to raise $\frac{E_f}{E_h}$, rather than on policy to raise and achieve the potential rate.

---

facilities for scientific education (and some people would say this is the situation in the UK) would have a low E_f, a high E_h, and a low E_f/E_h. Cf p. 30.

[1] It might be thought that tariffs (or an import surcharge) could keep the growth rates of imports and exports in line, at the cost of some loss of the potential gains from trade made possible by comparative cost differences. A tariff (or import surcharge) would cause a *once for all* reduction in imports in the year it was imposed, but it would not be likely to reduce E_h in the long run. Then its imposition would permit temporary growth in excess of $\bar{G}$, but it would need to be increased to allow growth rates exceeding $\bar{G}$ to continue after its *once for all* effect was cancelled out by subsequent faster growth of imports than exports. Thus, only continuously rising tariffs (or a continuously rising import surcharge) could permit continuous growth at rates exceeding $\bar{G}$. Import quotas would reduce E_h to zero for the goods they were imposed on, but they would increasingly harm consumers' welfare as output increased. Tariffs, an import surcharge, or import quotas would all continuously reduce a country's real gains from trade, while growth was maintained at rates exceeding $\bar{G}$.

There is, however, a way out of the difficulty. It has been assumed up to now that the home country's prices rise at the same rate as foreign prices. A country can, however, almost always improve its current account if it can arrange for its prices to fall in relation to prices abroad. If the home country's prices fell 1% relatively to foreign prices, and the foreign *price* elasticity of demand for its goods was e_f while its *price* elasticity of demand for foreign goods was e_h, its current account would improve by exports $\times(e_f-1)$% plus imports $\times e_h$%,[1] or by imports $\times(e_f+e_h-1)$% if exports equalled imports initially. Then a fall in its prices relative to foreign prices would lead to an improvement in its current account provided (e_f+e_h-1) exceeded zero as it certainly would for a developed economy.[2] It could then grow at its potential rate, even if this exceeded $\bar{G}$, provided it could arrange for a sufficient annual fall in its prices relatively to foreign prices.

If its potential growth rate exceeded $\bar{G}$ by 1%, and it actually grew at its potential rate, its imports would grow E_h% faster than its exports. Since a 1% fall in its prices relatively to foreign prices would improve its current account by imports $\times(e_f+e_h-1)$%, it could correct the E_h% per annum rise in imports due to 1% faster growth if its prices fell $\frac{E_h}{(e_f+e_h-1)}$% per annum relatively to foreign prices. Then a country's prices need to fall relatively to foreign prices by $\frac{E_h}{(e_f+e_h-1)}$% per annum for each per cent by which its potential growth rate exceeds $\bar{G}$—and they can be allowed to rise by $\frac{E_h}{(e_f+e_h-1)}$% per annum for each per cent by which $\bar{G}$ exceeds its potential growth rate. For the UK, it has been estimated that

[1] The demand for its goods abroad, and, *in the long run*, the quantity it sells there rises e_f%, but they are sold at prices which are 1% lower, so the money obtained from selling them rises only (e_f-1)%. At the same time, foreign goods (which are sold at unchanged prices) become 1% dearer relatively to home produced goods, so imports fall (in quantity and money cost) by e_h%.

[2] It is generally agreed that the price elasticity of demand for most manufactured goods exceeds 1, and developed economies export mainly manufactured goods. Then a developed economy's e_f would exceed 1, both because it exported manufactured goods, and because its goods competed with the manufactured goods of other developed economies which would make its e_f still larger.

E_h is 0·9, e_f $2\frac{1}{2}$ and e_h $1\frac{1}{2}$,[1] and with these figures, a 0·3% fall in UK prices relatively to foreign prices would permit 1% extra growth by the UK.

Of course, a fall in home prices relatively to foreign prices is not costless, and a 1% fall means that a country must export 1% more to obtain the same quantity of imports as before. If T is the proportion of GNP traded, it must give up T% of its GNP whenever its prices fall relatively to foreign prices by 1%. It is not then obvious that allowing a country's growth rate to rise from $\bar{G}$ to its potential rate by arranging for a fall in its prices relatively to foreign prices would increase the goods available to its population. More goods might be lost through the change in relative prices than those gained through faster growth. If the growth rate exceeded $\bar{G}$ by 1% per annum, the quantity of goods available would be raised by 1% per annum less any losses due to changes in relative prices. For a growth rate exceeding $\bar{G}$ by 1%, home prices would need to fall relatively to foreign prices by $\frac{E_h}{(e_f+e_h-1)}$% per annum, and this would cost the country $\frac{E_h}{(e_f+e_h-1)}.T$% of its GNP per annum. Thus the country would gain 1% extra goods per annum through faster growth, and lose $\frac{E_h}{(e_f+e_h-1)}.T$% per annum because it sold more cheaply abroad, i.e., it would gain $\left(1-\frac{E_h}{(e_f+e_h-1)}.T\right)$% per annum.[2] For the UK, T is about $\frac{1}{5}$, and if $\frac{E_h}{(e_f+e_h-1)}$% is 0·3%, it would gain 0·94% per annum from 1% faster growth. If these estimates are approximately correct, the UK would gain substantially from faster growth made possible by falls in its prices relatively to foreign prices. For every £100 worth of goods obtained through a faster growth rate than $\bar{G}$, only £6

[1] M. FG. Scott has estimated that the UK's income elasticity of demand for imports is 0·9, and its price elasticity of demand for imports $1\frac{1}{2}$. *A Study of UK Imports*, Cambridge University Press, 1963, pp. 49–51. A. J. Brown has estimated that the elasticity of *substitution* between UK exports of manufactured goods, and the manufactured exports of other nations (which is virtually the price elasticity of demand for UK exports) is $2\frac{1}{2}$. 'The fundamental elasticities in international trade', in *Oxford Studies in the Price Mechanism*, p. 97.

[2] Cf Professor H. G. Johnson's, *International Trade and Economic Growth*, Allen and Unwin, 1958, Chapter 3.

worth would need to be sacrificed through the fall in prices relatively to foreign prices needed to allow export earnings to rise at the same rate as import costs.[1] Similarly, with these figures, if the UK's $\bar{G}$ exceeded its potential growth rate by 1%, its prices could rise more than foreign prices, and this would increase its real incomes by 0·06% per annum.

It has been argued up to now that a country with a potential growth rate that exceeds its $\bar{G}$ will be unable to realise it without continuous deterioration in its current account, unless it can arrange for its prices to fall relatively to foreign prices. It has been suggested that the country's gains through extra growth might well substantially outweigh any losses due to the necessary fall in home prices relatively to foreign prices. It is now time to consider how the country could arrange for its prices to fall relatively to prices abroad, because this must be arranged if its long run growth rate is to exceed $\bar{G}$.

A country can do little to influence foreign prices, so its main influence over relative prices would need to be through control of the price level at which it sold to foreigners. It would need to arrange for its prices (in terms of foreign currency) to rise less than foreign prices. With fixed exchange rates, there would be little the country could do to influence the prices at which it sold to foreigners, because control of the domestic price level is notoriously difficult. It could be argued that the country's prices would rise less quickly if it had a faster growth rate (without excess demand), so faster growth itself might provide the solution to the problem.

[1] If $\frac{E_h}{(e_f+e_h-1)}.T\%$ was close to 1, another complication would need to be taken into account. Faster growth of 1% per annum would be unlikely to lead to greater output of consumer goods of 1% per annum, because a higher share of investment would generally be needed to achieve it. The annual increase in consumption which would follow in the long run from 1% faster growth would be 1% less the extra investment necessary for 1% faster growth and less the $\frac{Eh}{(e_f+e_h-1)}.T\%$ loss through a fall in home prices relatively to foreign prices. If the estimate that the loss to the UK through changes in relative prices from 1% extra growth would be as little as 0·06% per annum was approximately correct, this complication would have little effect on the argument so far as the UK was concerned. Clearly UK consumers would be better off in the long run if £100 of extra goods could be obtained through extra growth, even though £6 worth of these had to go to foreigners to allow exports and imports to balance at the faster growth rate, and even though some of the remaining £94 worth had to be capital rather than consumer goods.

The annual rate at which wage costs per unit of output rise, P, is the annual rate of increase in wages per worker, W, less the annual rate of increase in productivity, Q, i.e., P=W−Q. Then if Q rose as a result of faster growth of productivity, P, which equals W−Q, might fall. If prices rose with wage costs per unit of output so that P was also the rate of price inflation, faster growth in productivity would reduce P if it did not lead to an equal rise in W. To overcome the adverse effect of 1% faster growth on the current account which was outlined above, it would need to reduce P by $\frac{E_h}{(e_f+e_h-1)}$%, i.e., by 0·3% in the UK if the above estimates were correct. It is very difficult to know whether 1% faster growth would reduce the pace of inflation by 0·3% in the UK. Inflation in the UK between 1945 and 1964 was generally faster in periods when growth was faster, but growth was not obtained without excess demand, and the rate of inflation in different periods was much influenced by the rate at which import prices rose, so it is not clear whether faster growth itself increased or reduced price inflation. It is much clearer that the UK's current account improved in periods of zero growth, for instance, 1956–8 and 1961–2 (when there was obviously no excess demand), and this suggests that slow growth was helpful on balance to the UK's current account, so the cost reducing effect of faster growth was probably insufficient to outweigh its import increasing effect in the UK. Of course, in other conditions or other countries, faster growth might have a cost reducing effect which outweighed its import increasing effect, and the current account would then be more favourable with fast than with slow growth. A country in this fortunate situation would have the most favourable possible current account if it grew at its potential rate, so policy to raise and realise its potential growth rate would not conflict with policy to maintain balance of payments equilibrium. In the analysis below, the case of a country such as the UK which is probably not in this fortunate situation, will be considered.

It might be argued for a country in this less fortunate situation that an Incomes Policy could reduce its rate of inflation with consequent beneficial effects on its export prices. However, an Incomes Policy would only provide limited flexibility. It might not reduce the rate of inflation at all,[1] and even a successful Incomes

[1] Sweden and the Netherlands have had Incomes Policies since 1948, and they have not had significantly less inflation than the UK.

Policy would only be likely to reduce it to 1–2% per annum—few of its advocates would claim more than this—and this might not lead to a significant annual fall in home prices relatively to foreign prices, since many countries without Incomes Policies have only 1–2% inflation per annum. Even a successful Incomes Policy might therefore be inadequate where a country required a significant annual fall in home prices relatively to foreign prices for growth at its potential rate. On the other hand, a surplus country, i.e., a country with a $\bar{\bar{G}}$ exceeding its potential growth rate, which tried to maintain price stability through an Incomes Policy would cause its current account surplus to grow even more rapidly to the extent that the Policy was successful. This would cause it to accumulate unnecessarily large reserves and so increase the trading difficulties of other countries, and the surplus country would sacrifice the extra consumption it could otherwise have obtained through rises in its prices relatively to foreign prices. Thus an Incomes Policy *which aimed at price stability* might well provide insufficient flexibility for deficit countries, and its effect would be the opposite of that needed by surplus countries. This is not to suggest that an Incomes Policy would have no part to play in policy to maintain growth at the potential rate. In the absence of successful policy to limit price inflation, a country which needed falling prices relatively to prices abroad might have more inflation than other countries. It would then be unable to grow at its potential rate, both because its critical growth rate was less than its potential rate, and because its prices rose more than foreign prices when the opposite of this was necessary. Its actual growth rate would then be doubly reduced by the need to maintain current account equilibrium. Policy to limit inflation to the minimum possible, which might include an Incomes Policy, would then have an important role to play in deficit countries, but it might well be insufficient by itself (since it might merely prevent home prices from rising relatively to foreign prices) to make growth at the potential rate possible.

A more effective way in which a country could alter the prices of its goods relatively to prices of foreign goods would be through alterations in its exchange rate. An annual 1% depreciation of a country's exchange rate would apparently reduce its export prices relatively to foreign prices by 1% per annum. Thus a sufficient annual depreciation of its exchange rate could cause the annual fall in home prices relative to foreign prices which it needed for growth at its potential rate.

Suppose the exchange rate was free to fluctuate upwards or downwards by up to ¼% each month, or 3% per annum.[1] Then apparently home prices would be free to rise or fall (in terms of foreign currency) by up to 3% per annum. This is not quite the position. If the exchange rate depreciated 3%, home prices would be reduced 3% (in terms of foreign currency) if the home country's internal price level remained unchanged, while foreign prices (in foreign currency) would remain unchanged if foreign price levels remained unchanged. Home prices would then fall 3% relatively to foreign prices, if foreign and domestic price levels remained unchanged. It is, however, most unlikely that the domestic price level would remain unchanged if the exchange rate depreciated 3%. A 3% depreciation of the exchange rate would increase import costs 3% (in domestic currency) and this would increase overall costs by 3T% (where T is the proportion of trade to GNP). If T was $\frac{1}{5}$, the approximate proportion for the UK, 3% depreciation of the exchange rate would cause an immediate $\frac{3}{5}$% rise in home costs and probably therefore prices, and, with subsequent further cost push effects, an eventual price rise of perhaps 1%. If this was so, 3% depreciation of the exchange rate would reduce home prices relatively to foreign prices by perhaps 2%; 3% because of the fall in the exchange rate, less 1% because of consequent inflation. Flexibility in the exchange rate of up to 3% per annum would then allow flexibility in home prices relatively to foreign prices of up to 2% per annum. This might permit flexibility in, for instance, the UK's growth rate of up to 6·6% per annum.[2] This would mean that if the UK's $\bar{G}$ differed from its potential growth rate by less than 6·6%, a flexible exchange rate which was free to vary by 3% per annum might permit the annual change in home prices relatively to foreign prices needed for growth at the potential rate, if home prices would otherwise have risen at the same rate as foreign prices.

It might be thought that a flexible exchange rate would lead to uncertainty for exporters and importers, and that it would be an

[1] M. F G. Scott suggested this in 'What should be done about the Sterling Area?', *Bulletin of the Oxford University Institute of Statistics*, 1959.

[2] When the growth rate exceeds $\bar{G}$ by 1%, a fall in home prices relatively to foreign prices of $\frac{E_h}{(e_f+e_h-1)}$% is needed for current account equilibrium. If E_h is 0·9 in the UK, e_f 2½ and e_h 1½, a 0·3% change in relative prices is needed for 1% extra growth, so ±2% flexibility in relative prices per annum permits ±6·6% flexibility in the growth rate.

added stimulus to speculation. If a UK exporter could sell a motor-car in the US for \$2,800, and the exchange rate was fixed at \$2·80=£1, he would know that he could obtain £1,000 for the car. Then, if the cost of producing it was £900, he would know that his profit would be £100. If the exchange rate became \$2=£1 or \$4=£1 by the time the car was paid for, the exporter would receive £1,400 or £700 for the car, and make a profit of £500 or a loss of £200 depending on the exchange rate. This would make him uncertain whether it was worthwhile to export the car for \$2,800, and willingness to export and import would be much reduced. These harmful effects would follow if the exchange rate was free to fluctuate without limit,[1] and this is why it is suggested that limits of, perhaps, ¼% a month or 3% per annum should be set to permissible fluctuations. With such limits, the exporter would receive not less than £970 and not more than £1,030 if he was paid one year after the conclusion of the contract. Moreover, he could easily insure against fluctuation in the exchange rate by selling the promised \$2,800 for a fixed number of £s in the forward exchange market, and he could then export with certain knowledge of the £s he would receive.[2]

Trade would not then be hampered, because it would always be possible for exporters and importers to obtain forward exchange cover, but it might be thought that they would find the need for this an added expense. This would not necessarily be so. If there was fear that a country with a 'fixed' exchange rate might devalue,

[1] When the £ was flexible between 1931 and 1933, the exchange rate fluctuated between \$3·14½=£1 and \$5·53=£1 within twelve months which must have created considerable uncertainty for exporters and importers (see Sir Henry Clay, *Lord Norman*, Macmillan, 1957, pp. 404–6).

[2] If, for instance, the £ depreciated by 3% per annum relatively to the \$, and this was widely expected by foreign exchange dealers and traders, the forward premium on the \$ (and discount on the £) would be 3% per annum. The exporter could then sell the \$2,800 he would receive in a year's time for £1,030 to be received in a year's time. He would be absolutely certain of £1,030, because he could sell the \$2,800 he was certain to receive in advance to foreign exchange dealers, who would promise him £1,030 in a year instead of the £1,000 he would receive for a 'spot' sale of \$2,800. Similarly, a US manufacturer who sold a car for £1,000 in the UK and wished to be certain of a definite number of \$s, could sell £1,000 one year forward for 3% less than \$2,800, i.e., for \$2,716. Thus traders and manufacturers could either enter into *certain* contracts through the forward exchange market, or take the exchange risk themselves, and receive between £970 and £1,030 for a \$2,800 sale. Forward cover could also be obtained if the exchange rate fluctuated without limit, but it would then be much more expensive, and a large part of the real potential gain from trade might be lost.

traders would be aware of the possibility that future earnings in its currency might be reduced by up to 25%, and they would insure against this in the forward exchange market. It is not clear that it would be more expensive to insure against a likely fluctuation of up to 3% in a year than a possible fluctuation of up to 25%. It is also not clear that more speculative capital movements would be induced by likely annual exchange rate fluctuations not exceeding 3% than by possible fluctuations of up to 25%.

Because of the forward exchange market, there is then every likelihood that exchange rates with 3% flexibility per annum would permit continuous readjustment of domestic prices relatively to foreign prices, without particular inconvenience to manufacturers and traders. There would, however, be significant repercussions on the interest rate, and therefore possible repercussions on R and the potential growth rate itself. Suppose the UK's exchange rate (which is assumed to be \$2·80=£1 initially) depreciated 3% per annum, and that it was widely expected to do so. The forward premium on the \$ and discount on the £ would then be 3% per annum. Suppose also that Treasury Bill rates in both London and New York were 4%. If a US bank had £1,000 in London, it could convert it into \$2,800 at once and earn 4% interest on the \$2,800 in New York, i.e., \$112, and have \$2,912 at the end of a year. Alternatively, it could keep the £1,000 in London for a year, earn £40 interest, and expect to have £1,040 at the end of the year. It would, however, wish to be certain of a given number of \$s at the end of the year, so it would sell £1,040 forward for forward \$s at the beginning of the year. Because of the widely expected depreciation of the exchange rate, £s one year forward would sell for \$s at an exchange rate which was 3% less favourable than the 'spot' rate of \$2·80=£1, i.e., £1 one year forward would sell for \$2·716. Then the US bank would calculate that it would have \$2·716×1,040, i.e., \$2,824·64 at the end of the year if it left the £1,000 in London, as against the \$2,912 it would have if it transferred the money immediately to New York and earned 4% interest there. Then, if interest rates were the same in London and New York, most of the capital that could be shifted to New York would be, because it would be widely expected to appreciate 3% per annum in terms of £s there as well as earning 4% interest. This would make the UK's short term capital account unmanageable, and rapidly deplete its gold and foreign exchange reserves—making it impossible for the \$2·716=£1 exchange rate at the end of the year to be held.

To prevent this, the UK's Treasury Bill rate would need to be 3% higher than the US rate, i.e., it would need to be 7% if the US rate was 4%. Then, if the US bank left £1,000 in London, it would earn £70 interest in the year, and £1,070 could be sold forward for $2,906. With London interest rates 3% higher than New York rates, there would be no clear advantage in holding the £1,000 in the US. Consequently, holders of sterling balances would find it as advantageous to hold £s as $s, in spite of the depreciating exchange rate of the £. Then, if the exchange rate was widely expected to move against the £ by 3% per annum, London interest rates would need to be 3% higher than New York rates to prevent arbitrage which would otherwise make the UK's balance of payments unmanageable.

Of course, it is unlikely that full 3% depreciation of a currency would often be widely expected, but some currencies would be expected to depreciate and others to appreciate. A country with a potential growth rate exceeding its $\bar{G}$ would need falling home prices relatively to foreign prices and a depreciating exchange rate, and the foreign exchange market would come to expect this, and the country's currency would always then be at a discount in forward exchange markets. To maintain equilibrium in its short-term capital account, its short-term interest rates would need to be higher than those of other countries by the rate at which the forward exchange market expected its currency to depreciate. If the forward discount on the £ *vis-à-vis* the $ was 2% per annum (or ½% for three months), London interest rates would need to be 2% higher than New York rates.[1]

It might be thought that this would mean that an economy with a depreciating exchange rate would need to pay more interest to foreigners than an economy with 'fixed' exchange rates, but this is not necessarily so. Where a country's potential growth rate exceeds its $\bar{G}$ with 'fixed' exchange rates, its actual growth rate has to be restricted to $\bar{G}$, and it is likely to have balance of payments crises whenever its growth rate exceeds $\bar{G}$. The foreign exchange market will be aware that its currency might be devalued (by up to 25%) in one or other of these crises, and its exchange rate will therefore be at a continuous forward discount. There is no reason why the discount should necessarily be greater for a widely expected depreciation of up to 3% per annum, than for the

[1] See J. M. Keynes, *A Tract on Monetary Reform*, Macmillan, 1923, pp. 115–39.

possible depreciation of up to 25% which could be expected with 'fixed' exchange rates. Hence the interest which must be paid to foreigners might be no more with a depreciating flexible rate, than with a 'fixed' rate in which there was not complete confidence.[1]

However, whether the exchange rate is 'fixed' or flexible, a country's short-term interest rates must be higher than other countries' interest rates to the extent that its forward exchange rate is at a discount if equilibrium in its short-term capital account is to be maintained. This means that its government is apparently not free to fix its domestic interest rate independently of other countries' interest rates.[2] It could, of course, fix the interest rate as it pleased if it had a two-tiered interest rate structure, and paid higher interest rates to foreigners than to domestic lenders whenever this was necessary. Then, if the New York interest rate was 5%, and the forward discount on the £ 3% per annum, the UK government could pay 8% to foreign holders of sterling, and maintain a domestic interest rate of 4%. Very strict exchange control would be necessary for this, because UK residents could otherwise earn 5% interest, and 3% through appreciation of the $ if they could shift capital to New York, while they could only earn 4% in London. If effective exchange control of the necessary kind could be introduced and administered, a country could have a two-tiered interest rate structure, and it could then have a depreciating exchange rate, and complete freedom to use low interest rates to raise capital intensity at home.

The government would have no freedom to use interest rates to influence capital intensity in the absence of separate interest rates for home and foreign lenders. The interest rate would have to be the foreign interest rate, plus the annual forward discount of the

[1] In the period 1956–65, for instance, there was an almost continuous forward discount of the £ against the $, and it might well have been no larger than it actually was if the exchange rate had had 3% flexibility per annum.

[2] It might be thought that the UK authorities could fix whatever interest rate they wished, because they could fix the forward exchange rate through Bank of England intervention in the forward market. The Bank of England could regularly announce the forward exchange rate it would intervene to maintain. Then, the New York interest rate could be 5%, the London rate 4%, the £ depreciating 3% per annum *vis-à-vis* the $, and the £ at an annual premium of 1% in forward exchange markets because of Bank of England intervention. Here, anyone actually expecting 3% per annum depreciation of the £ could make a 4% per annum profit at the Bank of England's expense. The situation would also become particularly difficult for the Bank of England if the Federal Reserve Bank of New York announced it would intervene to maintain an annual forward $ premium of 2%.

currency, if massive capital account movements were to be avoided. In figure 7.1, the G_pG_p line shows what the potential growth rate would be at different interest rates.[1] The $\bar{G}\,\bar{G}$ line shows the relationship between the critical growth rate and the interest rate. A faster depreciation of the exchange rate of 1% per annum raises the critical growth rate (where imports and exports grow at the same rate)—in the case of the UK by perhaps 2·2%—and it might raise the necessary interest rate by 1%. Thus the interest rate has to be higher when $\bar{G}$ is raised (as a result of faster annual depreciation of the exchange rate), and the $\bar{G}\,\bar{G}$ line shows the necessary relationship between $\bar{G}$ and the interest rate.

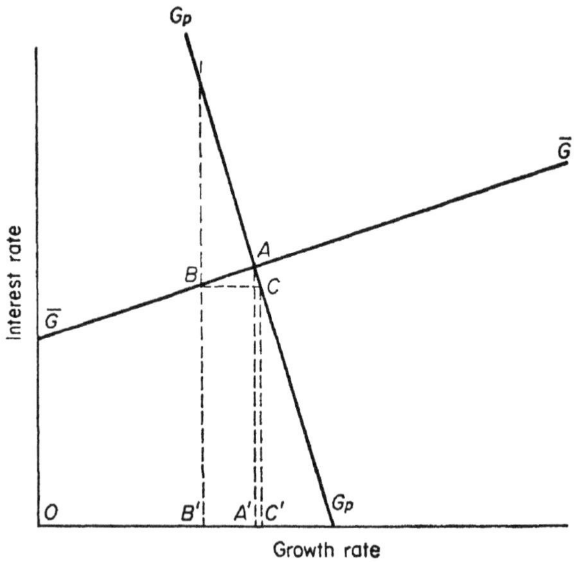

Fig. 7.1

The G_pG_p and $\bar{G}\,\bar{G}$ lines cut at A, and OA′ is then the fastest attainable growth rate, and AA′ the interest rate at that growth rate. A faster growth rate would be unattainable because a lower interest rate than AA′ would be needed to induce the capital intensity necessary for it, and this lower interest rate would be incompatible with the rate of depreciation of the exchange rate which would be needed at a faster growth rate.

[1] If the interest rate had no effect on the potential growth rate, i.e., no effect on R in the argument of Chapter 6, the G_pG_p line would be vertical, and there would be no danger that high interest rates (due to a depreciating exchange rate) would reduce the economy's potential growth rate.

The advantage of flexible exchange rates to an economy with a $\bar{G}$ which was less than its potential growth rate can easily be seen from this diagram. Suppose $\bar{G}$ is OB′ with fixed exchange rates *which are expected to remain fixed.* Then the interest rate is BB′, and the potential growth rate is OC′ at that interest rate. However, with a growth rate of OC′, imports would grow faster than exports, and the government would be forced to restrict the growth rate to OB′ to equate the growth of imports and exports. With flexible exchange rates, and falling home prices relatively to foreign prices, the interest rate would need to become higher than BB′ (though it would be higher than BB′ in any case if a fall in the exchange rate was anticipated before the switch to flexible rates), and this would reduce the potential growth rate and apparently be harmful to growth. This is, however, an illusion. With a higher interest rate of AA′, the potential growth rate, OA′, is indeed lower than the former potential growth rate of OC′, but it can actually be achieved, while the OC′ potential growth rate was an illusory one. With fixed exchange rates and a lower interest rate of BB′, only the low growth rate of OB′ is compatible with equal rates of growth of imports and exports. With flexible exchange rates, and the consequently higher interest rate of AA′, the growth rate which can actually be realised is raised from OB′ to OA′, and the reduced potential growth rate is now one which is compatible with long-run current account equilibrium.

Thus, to sum up the argument so far, flexible exchange rates, with limits to their flexibility of perhaps 3% per annum, might be the most promising means of equating an economy's potential growth rate to its critical rate. With a depreciating exchange rate, faster growth rates would be compatible with current account equilibrium, but interest rates might need to be higher making the potential growth rate lower. There would then be a particular growth rate which was compatible with a country's trade equilibrium and its economic potential, and this would be its fastest practicable growth rate. Flexible exchange rates would often be needed to allow a country to achieve this maximum potential growth rate in the long run.

There is a complication to the argument which does not affect its substance. It has been assumed up to now that the quality and composition of goods traded is given. Faster growth, however, might lead to more rapid redesign of products, speedier introduction of new products, and more rapid adjustment of a country's pattern of production to changing patterns of home and world demand. Then an increase in a country's growth rate might raise E_f, the foreign income elasticity of demand for its exports, and reduce E_h, its income elasticity of demand for imports. An increase in its *actual* growth rate might then increase $\frac{E_f}{E_h}$, and it would then increase $\bar{G}$ $\left(\text{which equals } G_f.\frac{E_f}{E_h}\right)$. If the change in $\frac{E_f}{E_h}$ was less than proportional to a change in G, the argument would be little altered. A growth rate faster than $\bar{G}$ would raise $\frac{E_f}{E_h}$, but it would raise it insufficiently to allow exports to grow as quickly as imports, and the faster growth rate could not then be sustained without a growing current account deficit. Because of the beneficial effect of growth on $\frac{E_f}{E_h}$, however, a smaller annual fall in home prices relatively to foreign prices would be needed by deficit countries than in the above argument, but some fall in relative prices would still be needed, so flexible exchange rates would still have a necessary part to play in policy for maximum long run growth.

If, however, the proportional change in $\frac{E_f}{E_h}$ was greater than the proportional change in G, an increase in G would always increase $\bar{G}$ by a greater amount. Faster growth (without excess demand) would then always lead to an improvement in the current account. This situation is analagous to the one mentioned earlier where 1% faster growth led to an improved current account if it reduced the pace of inflation by $\frac{E_h}{(e_f+e_h-1)}\%$ or more. In either of these situations, or in one where the combined effect of faster growth in lessening inflation and raising $\frac{E_f}{E_h}$ was sufficient, an economy's current account would be as favourable as possible when it grew at its potential rate, so the need for current account equilibrium would not conflict with policy to raise and realise its potential growth rate. With this state of affairs, flexible exchange rates would do no harm, and they would convert the current account surpluses which would follow faster growth into higher living standards instead of the accumulation of gold and foreign exchange reserves, but they would not be indispensable.

A country which was not in this fortunate situation, and the UK might well be one of these, would find it most difficult to maintain growth at its potential rate without flexible exchange rates. However, if it was unwilling to give its exchange rate limited flexibility for political or prestige reasons, it could perhaps experiment by maintaining growth at its potential rate for as long as possible. There would be an off-chance that this might lead to a sound current account as the pace of inflation, foreign demand, home supply, and the redesign of products and introduction of new products adjusted to faster growth, and its favourable effect might then be sufficient to outweigh its import increasing effect *in the long run*. It might turn out that the country's current account benefited from slow growth in the short run, and from fast growth in the long run; so its balance of payments might appear to be an obstacle to growth when the effect of rapid steady growth on its current account would actually be favourable.

8

CONCLUSION

As Keynes pointed out, prolonged growth could have a remarkable effect on output and living standards. In Chapter 1 it was remarked that continuous 2% growth would result in 624% growth in a century, and continuous 4% growth in 4,912% growth in a century. The argument of past chapters suggests that output could be increased more quickly than it has been in most developed economies. In the UK, for instance, growth has not been maintained at anything approaching the potential rate since 1900. Expansion has rarely been maintained without demand inflation, and attempts to get output to expand steadily without excess demand at rates close to the potential rate were generally unsuccessful. In consequence, growth was periodically halted altogether, and investment was much less than that needed for the potential rate. Growth also often had to be restricted to the *critical* rate compatible with trade equilibrium, because the exchange rate was fixed during much of the period, and there was no effective mechanism to reduce home prices relatively to foreign prices when this was necessary. Moreover, the potential growth rate which was not realised was itself lower than it might have been. There were tariffs on imported machinery during much of the period. Little attempt was made to ensure that there was sufficient research and development activity in industries (such as the machinery producing industries) where firms are too small to have adequate research departments. No real attempt was made to check restrictive practices until 1956. Profits (rather than 'pay-roll' or 'value-added') were taxed at high rates during much of the period, and investment incentives were only introduced in 1954. Thus the actually achieved growth rate was less than it might have been, both because the potential rate was less than it might have been, and because the actual rate must have been much below this low potential rate. In other developed economies, growth must also have been slower than it might have been for reasons such as these.

The actual rise in output per worker between 1900 and 1964 was 77% in the UK,[1] or 0·9% per annum. If the argument of past chapters is correct, policy to raise and achieve the potential growth rate along the lines suggested could raise future output per worker much more quickly than this. The UK's immediate growth target is 3·8% per annum, or a 3·4% growth rate in output per worker.[2] Opportunities for growth might well be sufficient to permit growth at this rate as against the 0·9% rate achieved between 1900 and 1964. In the remarks made below, it will be supposed that output per worker might grow 2% per annum in the next century. This is not to suggest that a 3·4% growth rate could not be maintained—even higher rates than this might well be practicable—but a 2% rate is one which would be widely agreed to be practicable, and even a rate as slow as this would have very startling effects by the year 2064.

In the past, real wages have risen at much the same rate as output per worker, so real wages might rise 624% between 1964 and 2064 if output per worker rose 2% per annum. In 2064, a worker in the UK might then earn £140 a week or £7,000 a year in place of the £18 10s. a week he earned in 1964. It might be thought that workers would then enjoy so high a standard of living that economic factors would cease to play an important part in life, but it is far from clear that this would be so.

£7,000 a year is a high income in the UK in the 1960's, and most people would find it adequate to meet every material need they wished to satisfy. In the 1960's it would allow a family to possess a house with a large garden in attractive surroundings, and to pay a gardener to look after the garden. It would allow a family to educate children in public schools where classes are small, to obtain domestic servants to assist with cooking, cleaning and looking after children, and to pay for expensive holidays and meals away from home, as well as providing for a wide range of manufactured goods. But £7,000 a year would only buy these things because over 99% of the population earn less than this.

If all workers had £7,000 a year, few could have houses in pleasant surroundings because there is insufficient space for many in a country the size of the UK. Since few are available, those that

[1] The British Economy. *Key Statistics 1900–64*. The Times Publishing Co., 1965, Table B.

[2] *The National Plan*, HMSO (Cmnd 2764), 1965, p. 2.

are will always be priced out of reach of the major part of the population. It would also never be possible for a worker to buy the direct labour of more than one other worker. If car workers' wages rose from £925 to £7,000 a year, the incomes of gardeners, waiters and schoolteachers would rise equally, and a car worker would be no more able to pay for much of their time when his income was £7,000 than when it was £925. Then the living standard available to someone with £7,000 a year in the 1960's would be completely out of reach of workers when everyone had £7,000. As workers became richer as a result of growth, everything which was not produced mechanically would rise in price at the same rate as their incomes, and much of what they wanted would always be too expensive for them. Moreover, if food became scarce in relation to population, it too would be so priced that only a minority of people could afford all they wanted. Thus, whether total output rose 624% or 4,912% in the next century, the great majority of people would be unable to afford many of the things they wanted, and unless a completely egalitarian society evolved, there would always be a minority who could afford the standard of living they wished for.

However, if this reasoning is correct, the economic system need never break down through lack of demand. If many workers always desired still higher incomes in the hope that they could obtain the things always priced out of their reach, tax reductions would always lead to higher spending, and governments could always increase demand when it fell below productive capacity by reducing taxes to reduce S. Thus, if the widespread use of automation led to saturation of the market for cars, cameras and mass produced clothes so that industrial employment fell, the government could increase people's spending power, and they would then shop more often where queuing was unnecessary and goods were delivered to their homes, eat out more, go for extra holidays, buy clothes which were not mass produced and spend more on domestic service. More employment opportunities would then be created in shops, hotels, restaurants, catering firms, tailoring, dress designing, and domestic service. In time, the proportion of the labour force employed in industry would fall, and the proportion providing personal services would rise, and as this process could continue indefinitely, automation need never cause unemployment.

Of course, if the proportion of the labour force employed in manufacturing steadily declined, the growth rate would very probably also decline, as there is more scope for increases in productivity through investment and technical advance in industry than in the occupations providing services. If productivity could be raised 4% per annum in industry, and only $\frac{1}{2}$% per annum in services, the overall growth rate of productivity would be 2$\frac{1}{4}$% when half the labour force provided services, 1$\frac{2}{3}$% when two-thirds provided services, and 0·85% when nine-tenths provided services. A 2% growth rate might not then be maintainable for a century, and a 624% rise in output per worker would not then be achieved by 2064, but growth would continue indefinitely, provided there was always some productivity growth in the provision of services—through the use and development of more mechanical aids in service occupations.

It might be wondered whether growth would really be of great benefit to people in a developed economy after production passed a certain point, since it would never make the mass of the population rich in the sense that a family with an income of £7,000 a year in the 1960's is rich. People would be able to buy almost unlimited quantities of material goods, but the possession and consumption of these might become subject to strong diminishing returns.[1] The increase in the quantity of material goods a worker could buy would become very great. In the UK in the 1960's a worker needs to work seven months to pay for a new small car—but with 624% overall growth in productivity and much faster growth than this in manufacturing because there would be less in services, he might only need to work a fortnight to possess a car, and seven months work might be sufficient to earn enough to buy a yacht or a helicopter. Workers would also be able to have much longer holidays and a shorter working week, and they would be able to spend their holidays in any part of the world. If working hours became

[1] Consumers lacking in self control might push consumption of particular goods well beyond the point where their pleasure from consumption of the good was maximum. They might, for instance, increase their consumption of cigarettes to the point where the satisfaction they obtained from an extra cigarette equalled the utility of the money required to buy it, but where their total satisfaction from smoking fell because the extra cigarette reduced the satisfaction obtained from other cigarettes smoked. A consumer with strong self control would avoid this danger by not increasing the number of cigarettes smoked beyond the point where his total satisfaction from smoking was maximum. Consumers with weak self control might destroy the satisfaction they obtained from many kinds of consumption through excess, and the frustrations which would follow from failure to find pleasure in consumption could have disquieting social effects.

shorter, they would need to devote less of their time and thought to routine work, and this would open up great opportunities for genuine education.

As the market for goods was saturated in developed countries, reluctance by their populations to assist underdeveloped countries might well become less, and willingness and ability to give aid could then be enormously increased. It is difficult to persuade the population of a country to give aid when its output is not growing, however high its living standard. People become accustomed to a certain living standard once it is achieved, and they may strongly resist attempts to reduce it. In the absence of growth, more goods can only be given to other countries (or to pensioners and widows) if the living standard of people at work is reduced. Aid and social services are then most easily extended in periods of growth when more can be given away without making anyone in the donor country worse off.

Clearly, if part of the benefit from 624% potential growth in a developed economy took the form of extra leisure, and additional aid to underdeveloped countries, wages would rise less than the 624% so far assumed, but they could still rise very substantially. Then, while prolonged growth would not allow all to enjoy as high a standard of living as they wished for, it would greatly raise material living standards, increase the help which could be painlessly given to underdeveloped countries, and increase leisure which would give people an opportunity to devote less time and thought to production and commerce. The use people made of their leisure would determine the fate of an affluent society.

INDEX

ANDREWS, P. W. S., 58n, 93n
Automation, 43–4, 168

BALANCE OF PAYMENTS, 30, 79, 107, 111, 116–17, 139, 148–65
Bauchet, P., 123n
Black, J., 7, 31n
Boulter, J., 7
Brittan, S., 128n
Brown, A. J., 153n
Butler, E. B., 7

CAPITAL INTENSITY
effect on growth, 27–8, 45–7, 54–5, 61–2, 66–70
factors influencing, 45–70, 84–90, 129–41
policy to influence, 54, 61–3, 129–47, 161–3
Capital, life of, 21–8, 31–4, 79–80, 101–3, 106–7
Capital output ratio, 10, 18–19, 43–4, 64n, 72–3, 84–90 (*see also* capital intensity)
marginal capital output ratio, 12, 17n, 40, 55, 62
Clay, Sir Henry, 158n
Cobb, C. W., 66–8
Cobb-Douglas production function, 66–70
Commisariat Général du Plan, 122–3
Costing margin, 93

DENISON, E. F., 36n
Department of Economic Affairs, 122
Depreciation, 10, 13, 18n, 49n, 70
Diminishing returns to capital, 11–13, 20, 66–8, 82
Dividends, 86
Douglas, Paul H., 66–8
Dow, J. C. R., 113n, 128n
Duesenberry, J., 73n, 86n, 126n

ECONOMIES OF SCALE, 17n, 19–21, 39, 66–8, 145
Education, 35–6, 42
Eltis, W. A., 42n, 64n, 94n, 140n, 144n
Entrepreneurial efficiency, 22–30, 51–4
European Common Market, 46
Excess capacity, 86–7, 91–3, 105, 110n, 129n, 135–9
Exchange rates, 156–65

FAULKNER, D. O., 8
Fellner, W., 11, 48n
Finance, supply of, 21–30, 57n, 117–21, 125–8
Fuel costs, 62–3

GALBRAITH, J. K., 38n
Gestation period, 55, 115
Growth, rate of,
actual, 10–11, 72–5, 104–14
critical, 149–65
expected, 114–17, 121, 125, 127–8
natural, 13–31, 77–97, 106–8
full natural, 17–21, 29–30
warranted, 72–97, 104–14

HABAKKUK, H. J., 46n, 50n
Harrod, Sir Roy, 7, 8, 10n, 11n, 13n, 16, 43n, 74n, 75–7, 79, 83–4, 106n, 108n, 113n, 122, 124n
Henderson-Stewart, Sir David, 8

INCOMES POLICY, 107, 155–6
Imperfect competition, 17n, 19–20, 145
Inflation,
  cost-induced, 60–1, 154–7
  demand-induced, 30, 78–81, 107–14, 139–40, 148, 155
Input–output matrix, 124
Interest, rate of, 14–19, 56–8, 93, 121, 134, 141–2, 159–63
Investment,
  effect on growth, 9–13, 16–34, 45–7, 54–5, 66–70
  factors influencing, 72–7, 98–141
  policy to influence, 98–147
Investment incentives, 101–3, 134, 143

JOHNSON, H. G., 153n

KAHN, R. F., 93n, 133n
Kaldor, N., 17n, 49n, 85n, 90n, 91n, 92n
Kalecki, M., 93n
Keynes, J. M., 9, 78n, 83, 93n, 99n, 160n, 166
Kuznets, S., 48n

LABOUR FORCE
  increase of, 14–17, 19n, 31–4
  scarcity of, 58, 88–9, 94–7
  skilled, 30, 42–3, 51, 150n
Lauderdale, James Maitland, 8th Earl of, 96

MACHINERY PRODUCING INDUSTRIES, 41–2, 52–4, 63–6
Maywald, K., 48n
Merrett, A. J., 117n
Mirrlees, James A., 17n, 85n
Monetary policy, 119–21, 127–8
Monopoly, 36–8, 40–2, 93, 134–5, 143

NATIONAL ECONOMIC DEVELOPMENT COUNCIL (*and* Office), 7, 103n, 122, 137n, 144n

OLIGOPOLY, 38, 40–1
Ordinary shares, 117–19

PAISH, F. W., 113n
Pay-roll taxation, 29n, 46, 54, 60–1, 142–3
Plan, The National, 167n
Planning, 20–1, 29, 121–5
Price flexibility, 90–6, 140n
Profit, rate of,
  effect on growth, 14, 17n, 46–7, 54–66, 84–90, 130–47
  factors influencing, 58–9, 84–90, 132–5
  policy to influence, 138–47
  notional rate of profit, 21–2, 85–6, 93, 130, 133–5
Profits,
  share of, in National Income, 66–8, 90–6, 140n
  taxation of, 29n, 60n, 120–1, 134, 142–3, 146–7
  undistributed, 86, 90, 118–21, 125–7

READING, B., 8
Research and development, 18, 36–42
Restrictive practices, 22, 39–40, 41, 93, 143
Ricardo, David, 55n, 65n
Richardson, G. B., 8
Richardson Committee, 142n
Risk, 14, 57n, 86–8, 130n, 134, 138
Robinson, Joan, 23n, 59n, 65n, 66n, 71n, 80n, 85n, 99n, 116n, 141, 146
Rostas, L., 49n, 63n
Rothbarth, E., 46n
Rudd, M., 8

SAVING, 30, 71–2, 77–82, 90–7, 122, 132–3, 138–40, 144–6
Schumpeter, J. A., 37n
Scott, M. FG., 8, 153n, 157n
Sen, A. K., 94n
Seton, F., 124n
Shone, Sir Robert, 61n, 62n, 122n, 129n
Solow, R. M., 85n
Steindl, J., 40n, 86n
'Stop-go', 107–17, 128
Sykes, A., 117n

TARIFFS, 50–4, 61, 151n
Technical progress,
effect on growth, 9, 14–33, 35, 68–9
factors influencing, 17–19, 27–8, 35–43, 45–54, 84, 131
policy to influence, 35–43, 129–47
embodied and disembodied, 15–16, 33, 35, 69
neutrality of, 43–4, 60

UNDERDEVELOPED ECONOMIES, 80
Unemployment, 31, 71–97, 105–6, 136, 168

VALUE-ADDED TAXATION, 29n, 142–3

WAGES, 46–54, 58–63, 66–8, 88–9, 90–6, 155, 167–70
Ward, P. E., 42n
Wicksell, K., 66n, 68
Wiles, P. J. D., 26n, 28n, 122n
Wilson, T., 58n
Wolfe, J. N., 8

YOUNG, ALLYN, 20n

For Product Safety Concerns and Information please contact our EU
representative GPSR@taylorandfrancis.com
Taylor & Francis Verlag GmbH, Kaufingerstraße 24, 80331 München, Germany

www.ingramcontent.com/pod-product-compliance
Ingram Content Group UK Ltd.
Pitfield, Milton Keynes, MK11 3LW, UK
UKHW021507240926
475702UK00035B/634